UNDERSTANDING CATHOLICISM

Understanding
CATHOLICISM

Monika K. Hellwig

PAULIST PRESS   *New York/Ramsey*

Library of Congress
Catalog Card Number: 81-80047

ISBN: 0-8091-2384-3

Published by Paulist Press
545 Island Road, Ramsey, N.J. 07446

Printed and bound in the
United States of America

Contents

To

THE JESUITS OF GEORGETOWN UNIVERSITY

TO WHOM I OWE
SO MUCH AND SO MUCH
I DEDICATE THIS BOOK
WITH ALL ITS FAILINGS
IN A SPIRIT OF
GRATITUDE
AFFECTION
AND GREAT ADMIRATION

Introduction
Faith and Understanding:
Sources and Resources

Some people worry when they have questions about their faith, or when they begin to realize that the old explanations, good enough before, no longer seem to offer coherent meaning. This worry is misplaced. To believe means to want to understand, and to want to understand means to be asking questions. To ask questions means to be uncertain, perhaps puzzled or perplexed.

To believe means to want to understand because faith is an orientation of one's thinking and of one's whole life. Faith is precisely the opening of one's mind, one's understanding to God revealing himself. But what God reveals to us is not apparent instantaneously, once and forever in all its implications. What God reveals is received or seen according to our present capacity. That capacity is shaped by our individual human maturity, by the maturity of our society and its culture and language, and also by our access to testimonies of God's self-revelation. Human beings grow to maturity slowly through all kinds of experiences which are never quite the same for any two people. Faith involves a continuing effort of personal appropriation and understanding. Human societies and cultures and languages also develop. There cannot, therefore, be a formulation of the faith of Catholics once and for always in such a way that it would save us from further reflection and efforts to understand. Every formulation of the content of our faith is more a starting point than a conclusion.

Besides all the above, our capacity to receive God's self-revelation in faith depends on our fundamental willingness to do so. Faith is the opening of one's mind and understanding to God revealing himself. But God's revelation exerts an exigence on the whole orientation of our lives. It is not really possible to open one's mind to the truth while excluding that truth from making claims on one's life. Even when one makes a wholehearted assent to God as he reveals himself, the global generosity that accepts all the implications is not enough. It does not substitute for the discovery, step by step, of what those implications are, and the acceptance of them one by one. We know this as a general rule in life. It is this way with a marriage, with the acceptance of a new child into a family and even with a new job. In principle, one accepts or agrees to whatever is involved. In practice this is only discovered little by little. It may be full of surprises and hold demands going far beyond anything anticipated. Under such circumstances the initial generosity often falters. One may have to make repeated efforts to come to a new and deeper understanding and to a new and deeper commitment. The understanding and the commitment are closely interwoven. To the extent that one is unready for the more radical commitment demanded, one is likely to find one's understanding of the situation clouded and confused.

This is certainly true of an individual's growth in faith in the course of life's experiences, surprises and disappointments. This is not difficult to see. What may be less obvious is that something similar happens in the life of the whole community, in the life of the whole Church in the course of the centuries. Individuals are not always fully open in faith to God's revelation. There are hesitations, infidelities and setbacks in the best of lives. Yet all are challenged to new and deeper awareness and new and deeper response by the experiences of their lives. The whole Church is made up of such individuals. As community, as Church, they are on a common journey toward deeper awareness and fuller response through their experiences in history. The common journey suffers along the way from the frailties of these individuals. The testimonies of faith that individuals receive come from imperfect people. The testimony they give may be clouded and confused.

The message of God's self-revelation in Jesus has come to each of us through a number of channels, none of which is free from human error and the ambiguities of history. What we learn from Scripture, for example, depends very much on how we have been taught to read and interpret Scripture. It also depends on the questions and expectations we have been taught to bring to the study of Scripture. We learn the teachings of the Church in certain formulations. But the formulations were originally made according to the language and experience available to the formulators. They depended on the depth of commitment to Christ and to the task of redemption of those formulators. This is obviously true of individual parents, teachers, preachers, theologians and other ministers of the word both now and in the past. But it is also true of councils of the Church and of great Popes and saintly bishops. They formulated as best they were able with the language, experience and degree of commitment and understanding available to them. Of course the Spirit of God prompted and sustained them. However, the work of the Spirit, which is the power of grace, is to liberate human creativity, not to crush it or substitute for it.

The history of the Church suggests that God is very patient waiting for human response and human understanding. God empowers human creativity and waits for revelation and salvation to be received in a human way. Therefore there are really no statements or formulations in which God has given us a final answer or explanation in words. Each formulation comes from a particular social and cultural situation. Language and experience and social structures change, and with them the demands of implementing the Gospel necessarily change. For this reason, even the most solemn statement of a council or the solemn (*ex cathedra*) pronouncement of a Pope is more a starting point than a final answer. This does not deny the infallibility of the Church or the specific doctrine of the infallibility of certain solemn papal pronouncements. Rather it accepts it as meaningful in the larger context of a world that develops and changes. This is discussed further in Chapter 7 of this book. The point here is that no formulation, solemn and official though it be, can cancel the task of further reflection from the living experience of believers.

However, this task of reflection, this wanting to understand, can only be pursued by asking questions. They are far-reaching questions, dangerous questions, frightening questions. They are dangerous and frightening in two ways. First of all they may show that the Gospel of Jesus Christ is really much more demanding than we had previously thought. Secondly, they may seem to be taking us away from the tradition and the authorities on which our faith rests. It is obvious that the first risk must be taken. The second is of a different kind and calls for hesitation and deliberation. Clearly one must ask questions, but they ought to be the right questions asked the right way. This may make the difference between a genuine quest for understanding within the faith on the one hand and a gradual abandoning of the faith on the other.

Questions may be asked petulantly with the intention to rebel and undermine and destroy. On the other hand, they may be asked with the intention to participate in a project more intelligently, to support, to solve problems, to cooperate more fully. This is true both of questions that ask why and of those that ask how. It is true of those that ask whether and of those that ask when. Many Catholics today are fearful of questioning because they have heard so much of it done petulantly, rebelliously, in anger. We hear more of this because this kind of questioning is spectacular enough to be newsworthy for the press. It should not be forgotten that the other kind of questioning, which seeks deeper understanding in order to cooperate more fully, is going on all the time, though it only reaches the news media when there is a misunderstanding, a sharp disagreement, or perhaps a book that reaches the best seller list. This other kind of questioning is the professional work of theologians. However, it is also the unavoidable task of every Christian whenever new situations and experiences arise.

The questions that deepen faith rather than destroy it move in two directions. Some begin with questions out of present experience and ask what light traditional Christian doctrine can shed on these matters. Much moral theology must move in that direction. There are urgent questions having to do with the public, political and economic dimensions of morality and those having to do with realms in which we now know more or have more technical power. Sometimes questions of belief move in this direction also. More often they move in the opposite direction. They begin with traditional formulations of faith from the past and ask what meaning these have for Christians today. They seek for the meaning of traditional doctrines in terms of the experiences, decisions and challenges facing us today. This book is concerned with questions that move in this latter direction.

There are many ways to ask about the meaning of traditional formulations of faith for the contemporary Christian. The matter can be studied with cool detachment from outside the commitment by historians of religion or cultural anthropologists. These are interested simply in finding out what interpretations and adaptations believers have made. They are not interested in judging whether the adaptations are good or bad, the interpretations true or false. However, the whole matter can also be approached with the conviction that truth claims are important, that there is a thread of continuity, and that the true meaning is discovered by the guidance of the Spirit in the Church. One might call this the committed quest for the contemporary meaning because it is carried on within the commitment of and to the Church.

The characteristically Catholic way of carrying on a committed quest sees Church tradition as the principal source of Christian doctrine and its understanding. The Bible holds a central place within this tradition. It does not stand in isolation as a separate source of Christian doctrine. It is the book (or collection of writings) of the believing community of the beginning and of their Jewish precursors. It is the book of the Church, the whole Church of all ages. Its meaning is in the keeping of the Church, the whole Church of all ages. But the Bible is unique in the "library" of the Church. There is a polarity or tension between the text set down in the beginning on the one hand and the understanding of the text by the living Church on the other. The text is dependent on the Church for interpretation but it also confronts and challenges the Church in all its failures of faith and understanding.

Church tradition has crystallized Christian doctrine in other texts besides those that make up the Bible. From earliest times, local churches and councils have composed creeds, also known as confessions or symbols of faith. Some have served their purpose and faded into disuse. Others have remained as a permanent part of the heritage. Examples of the latter are the Apostles' Creed and the Nicene Creed (which is actually the Niceno-Constantinopolitan creed). From a Catholic perspective, there can be no effort at the contemporary understanding of the Christian faith that does not refer to these official creeds as well as to the biblical text. But besides the creeds, there are other official texts of worship, some very old. These include texts for the celebration of the Eucharist, for the sacraments of initiation and for the ordination of deacons and presbyters. The content of the prayer of the churches is always the content of the faith of the churches.

Some of the most important formal declarations and explanations of the faith by the great councils of the Church were built on this last principle. The Catholic understanding of the faith is heavily indebted to four councils held in the fourth and fifth centuries—Nicea in 325 A.D., Constantinople in 381 A.D., Ephesus in 431 A.D., and Chalcedon in 451 A.D. These laid the dogmatic foundations of Christology, that is, of the understanding of the identity and meaning of Jesus. There were several important councils of antiquity after these four, but by the time of Chalcedon a vocabulary and a line of argument had been set which have continued to provide a frame of reference for Catholic efforts to understand the implications of the Christian faith. These early councils provide the classic explanation of how Jesus of Nazareth is pivotal in history and in the human relationship to the transcendent God. He is a man sharing our humanity. Therefore we can imitate him, join in his life project and empathize with him. He is at the same time, in ways beyond our scrutiny, empathy and imagination, uniquely Son of God, sharing the divinity of the Father. Therefore we can worship him and place unconditional trust in him.

Since the eleventh century there has been a tragic schism between the churches of the East, which spoke mainly Greek, and the churches of the West which spoke Latin. For the Western churches, however, councils did not end with that schism. The Catholic Church of today traces the continuity of its history and its link with the apostles through these churches. The Catholic tradition, therefore, acknowledges as authoritative a series of medieval and modern councils, dealing, among other things, with authority in the Church, salvation and the sacraments. A further tragic schism at the time of the sixteenth-century Reformation split the churches of the north from those of the south in Western Europe. Even after this, the churches remaining united with Rome met three more times in council. This was at Trent, 1545–1563, at Vatican I, 1869–1870, and at Vatican II, 1962–1965. These modern councils range over a much wider spectrum of questions and go into some of them in very much more detail than the ancient or the medieval councils. They also have become an official source for Catholic efforts to understand the Christian faith.

It may seem from the above that it should be easy to compile the official teaching of the Catholic Church, at least in its councils. This, however, is not really any easier than compiling the doctrinal teachings of the Bible. In both cases we have a collection of documents written over a span of centuries by a great variety of authors. They are taken from a wide range of previous oral traditions and are set within a full spectrum of different cultures, languages and historical experiences. One cannot set such statements side by side as part of the same explanation. Often they seem to be in outright contradiction of one another. At other times it is not clear whether they are really addressing the same question. Nor is it always evident what is the worldview and frame of reference that undergirds both questions and answers. Simply to establish a clear account of what has been officially taught is a first step in the task of theology before anyone can reflect on its meaning for us today. Yet it always turns out to be more than a task of compiling. It cannot be separated from the task of interpretation.

Besides the statements and definitions of the councils, the official and formal teaching of the Church also includes a far more elusive body of testimonies. There is the standard and continuing teaching of the bishops as leaders and guides of the churches when they are not met in council. A single letter or the instruction of a single bishop does not of itself carry much weight for the whole Church. But the bishops represent the local churches and their traditions. Therefore the cumulative sense or import of what has heen taught by the bishops is an important testimony to the content of the Christian faith. Of particular importance in this body of testimonies are written and published statements of the Popes. These include papal encyclicals (letters sent around to all the local churches) and key speeches and sermons officially released for publication.

Among the utterances of the Popes, one category enjoys a privileged status, the type of pronouncement known as *ex cathedra,* solemnly pontifical. These are statements which claim to stand with the definitions of the councils. They are official interpretations of the revelation that the Church has received in Jesus Christ. They claim to be treated as definitive and irreformable. This category is not in practice an important resource for ascertaining the teachings of the Catholic Church, because it appears that only two papal statements have really made the claims that put them in this category. Both of these related to Marian doctrine.

There is also a large and shadowy periphery of papal teachings. This consists of pronouncements of "the Holy See" not coming from the Pope in person but from many congregations, commissions and offices making up the Vatican staff. These cannot be ignored as a source of Catholic teaching, but they complicate the task immensely by their multiplicity, complexity and detail. They also speak from different frames of reference depending on the areas of expertise from which the members of these bodies are drawn. Obviously, not all statements are to be given equal importance, but in practice the hierarchy of their authority is by no means clear. Again, there can be no question of simply compiling. They call for a skilled task of interpretation in the light and context of the tradition as a whole.

Three major resources have been discussed so far. These are the Bible, the creeds and liturgical texts, and the conciliar, episcopal and papal teachings. They are the explicit and official part of the Catholic heritage, and are easily identifiable. There is also a counterpart which is unofficial, more diffuse, less easily identifiable and often less explicit. This counterpart is actually more fundamental. Through the centuries the official formulations have grown out of it, and they continue to do so. Yet the official formulations in turn influence the further shaping of the unofficial part of the heritage.

This other aspect consists of the Christian life of the community of believers. It consists of their faith that gradually receives and appropriates God's self-revelation in their lives and their communities. It consists of their hope that shapes itself according to the Gospel as heard in the context of the particular circumstances of their lives. It consists of their practical charity as they find the responses, actions, attitudes and life-styles appropriate to their faith and hope. This is the matrix or flow of Catholic tradition out of which official formulations are distilled from time to time. The words of those formulations really have no content other than by reference to the living and lived reality.

Between the living flow of the Christian community and the official formulations there is a wealth of literature and art that plays a mediating function. These works express Christian experience, longings and convictions in many ways. Some are more spontaneous, others more reflective and critical. Some are more imaginative and poetic, others argued more rationally or discursively. This vast resource includes Christian art and architecture, music, poetry, drama and fiction. It also includes much biography and autobiography, sermons and meditations and more systematic reflections on the Christian spiritual life. It includes letters, instructions and rules that set out a way of life for voluntary groups. It includes systematic attempts to explore Christian faith, or to explain or defend it. It also includes works more specifically concerned with the Catholic understanding or practice of the Christian life, or even with some more specialized tradition within it. There are arguments over orthodoxy, which is the rightness of beliefs, and over orthopraxis, which is rightness of behavior. There is much more besides these.

This body of texts and other records is a very important resource in the understanding of the Catholic faith. But it is also vast, diffuse and difficult to define concretely. Efforts have been made to collect some parts of it. For the early ages of Christianity we have great collections of the writings of the "Fathers of the Church." These are witnesses to the faith and thought and life of the early churches. They have been officially recognized as a source for Catholic theology and the determining of Tradition on particular issues. (Spelled with the capital letter, Tradition means the orthodox teaching that ought to be handed down.) The Church has also established a process of canonization of saints. This pinpoints the recollection of certain lives and the telling of their stories as a means of understanding the implications of the faith. Official approval of religious congregations and movements, along with their rules and spiritual teachings, places these explicitly within the heritage of Catholic tradition. Further, the collection and editing of spiritual writings from various schools and traditions have proved helpful to successive generations of readers. These are often reflected in later official teaching.

These are the sources for any understanding of the Catholic faith in its relevance and its exigency for our lives today. One may question the meaning of the formal teachings only in the context of the living faith community and its vast heritage of unofficial testimonies and records.

Related Material

The official teachings of the Catholic Church have been semi-officially collected in the original languages (usually Latin, occa-

sionally Greek) in Enchiridion Symbolorum *of Heinrich Denzinger, edited in its thirty-third edition by Adolf Schönmetzer, for Herder (Freiburg). Much of this material is available in translation in* The Teaching of the Catholic Church *by Joseph Neuner and Heinrich Roos (Alba House).*

There are many series of the Fathers of the Church in translation—for instance, the Ancient Christian Writers series (Newman Press). A more comprehensive presentation of Catholic teaching including worship, beliefs and way of life is the two-volume Catholicism *by Richard McBrien (Winston Press). Introductory presentations of creeds, key beliefs, sacraments and the process of tradition are available in four short books:* The Christian Creeds: A Faith To Live By, The Meaning of the Sacraments, Tradition, the Catholic Story Today, *and* What Are the Theologians Saying? *by Monika Hellwig (Pflaum Press).*

Further bibliography is given at the end of each chapter and in the references mentioned above.

I

Human Life
Before God

1

God Revealed
as Powerful Compassion

Catholic faith rests upon the conviction that we, the human race, are, not alone in a void of meaninglessness. Whether or not we know it, we live our lives and make our history "from" and "in" and "to" a caring and compassionate God. For this reason everything in human experience is important. Everything is to be integrated in the focus of life to God, and therefore everything is to be judged in the light of an ultimately serious purpose. There is no profane or secular realm of matters that are indifferent to the final purpose and can therefore go their own way. There are no experiences or actions, joys or sufferings, achievements or failures, satisfactions or disappointments too trivial to be integrated in the focus of life to God.

Catholic faith rests upon the conviction that we know this with utter certainty not because it can be demonstrated like a scientific experiment or a piece of historical research, nor because we can argue to it by the speculations of philosophers, but because God has revealed (unveiled) himself for us to see, has touched us for us to feel his presence, has called us so that we might recognize the voice and realize that we are known by name and greatly valued and cherished. We claim that we know this through Jesus of Nazareth and his impact on those around him which has sent ripples down the centuries through the whole human community. This claim is true, but historically we can take it further back than Jesus into the experience of the people of Israel which Jesus himself inherited.

The people of Israel have given an account of their experience and their wisdom in a heritage that consists largely of stories and poetic imagery. Many of these stories have to do with revelation, that is, the self-revelation of God. The idea of revelation is not in the first place a purely religious one. As a matter of common experience, we use the word in daily life. We may say about an encounter with a person, about a tragic or particularly happy event, about a beautiful scene or about our own or someone else's insight that it came as a revelation or that it was a revelation. Reflecting on this, we become aware that what we mean by calling something revelatory is that it has a certain quality of being experienced as a gift rather than something earned or rightfully due. In keeping with this giftlike quality a revelation in this everyday sense seems to involve an element of surprise though not necessarily suddenness. The content of such revelations is some sort of new knowledge or insight or understanding. Usually this is not so much a matter of additional information as a breakthrough in the manner or depth or intimacy with which something or someone is known.

When we speak of revelation in a religious sense, we are still using the word in more or less the same sense of a breakthrough experience in insight, knowing and understanding that takes us by surprise and introduces us to a new dimension of depth and intimacy with the ultimate, the One, the source and foundation and goal of our being. This kind of breakthrough can happen in a number of different ways: in our experiences of nature, in the workings of our own conscience and consciousness, in personal relationships with other people, and in the history of the community.

The most basic and universally available kind of revelatory experience in the religious sense is the one associated with an experience of nature. Most of us have at one time or another been flooded by a sense of power, beauty, majesty or mystery at the sight of great mountains, vast sweeps of sky, the immense ocean with its rhythmic waves, the stillness of lakes, the blanketing quiet of forests. Most of us have at some time had a sense of an encompassing providence in spring sunshine, winter snow, autumn's brilliant colors, summer's extravagant abundance of life, the wonder of birth and the balm of sleep. These and so many other experiences, not all joyful ones, offer the opportunity for the revelation and discovery of the all-encompassing power and presence of the One who is greater than we are, prior to us, transcending our ability to grasp, our bountiful host in the world of nature, the silent but welcoming backdrop to all our experiences of life. The Hebrew Scriptures (known to most Christians as the Old Testament) are full of allusions to such experiences, suggesting them as starting points for our prayer that will lead us to deeper encounters with the transcendent, hidden but ever-present God. Such allusions form a constant theme, for instance, in the psalms, Jewish prayers which Christians continued to pray from the earliest Christian times, as indeed Jesus himself did.

More subtle but just as universal is the discovery of God revealing himself in the inner depths of our own conscience and consciousness. This happens in the emergence of a moral exigence that demands that we seek what is right above self-interest—the moral exigence that leaves us discontent with all that is not truthful, not authentic, not just, unmerciful or evasive. In the same way it happens in the discovery of human transcendence, the power to rise above situations and transform them, inner resources of strength and creativity. In these we experience ourselves as drawn or called by a power above and far ahead of us, and yet a power that is intimately involved in creating us, summoning us to be more than we are. This theme, too, we find in the psalms and in the great prophets of Israel, such as Isaiah and Jeremiah. We also find many testimonies to such experiences in Christian literature, probably none more powerful or moving than some of the introspective parts of the *Confessions* of St. Augustine of Hippo who lived in the late fourth and early fifth century.

In most of our lives, however, we are probably far more conscious of the discoveries that we make, the revelations that open up for us, in our relationships with other people. In the love of other people we discover our own worth and dignity and meaning in life, and this can easily open out on a self-revelation of God who creates us out of love. In the limitations of all our relationships we discover that we are made for something far beyond any of these, and that also is a self-revelation of God if we are open to it. But it is perhaps most of all in the experience of parenthood that God is revealed in our own growing capacity for empathy, compassion, acceptance and creative cherishing of others, bringing them out of nothingness. The analogy of the human love of spouses and parents for the creative and redeeming fidelity of God that is revealed to us is a favorite one in the Hebrew Scriptures. The prophets frequently dwell on it, and the psalms allude to it from time to time. The New Testament takes over the theme in some of the sermons and parables of Jesus.

Revelation is found further in the history of the community, and this is where it becomes formulated in special religious language. For Israel the foundation event in the self-revelation of God was the exodus, and this shaped all subsequent perception and language in their encounters with the presence of God in their history. The God who reveals himself is the liberator of Israel, and the liberator of the human person; he is one who sum-

mons people to freedom out of bondage, to peoplehood out of
a herd of frightened self-protective individuals, and to a purpose
in life out of an aimless existence. The Christian understanding
of God's self-revelation in Jesus also carries over the exodus imagery and story which have helped to shape Christian theology.

The meaning and content of revelation are expressed by Israel in a number of stories, of which the most striking is that of
the burning bush. This story illuminates what we mean by revelation in our Christian faith which rests so heavily on ancient
Hebrew experience and on the Bible. In the story of the burning
bush Moses is at a critical point in his life. A member of an oppressed class by birth, he has been exempted from the suffering
of the oppressed by being adopted into the royal household but
has nevertheless identified himself passionately with them as an
adult. This has brought him into trouble so that he has fled and
is now an exile. As he herds sheep on a lonely mountain slope,
a vision appears before his eyes of a bush that burns but is not
consumed. He becomes aware that he is being called by name.
When he responds and comes closer he is warned to approach
with great reverence, taking his shoes off, and then learns that
it is the God of his (desert nomad) ancestors, Abraham, Isaac
and Jacob, who calls him. He also learns that he is called to a
task far beyond his strength and capabilities which this God will
accomplish in him. The task is the liberation of the utterly oppressed Hebrews for whom God is moved to deep compassion.

One might at first think that such a story has an almost magical ring to it. At the very least twentieth-century readers would
certainly not expect any experiences like this to happen in their
own lives. Moreover, they might very well think that if some
thing like this did happen they would certainly have to believe
that there is someone, some One, behind the scenes of our everyday experience manipulating the affairs of the world. More
careful reading and reflection in the light of the whole of Scripture and in the light of Jewish interpretations of this passage

suggests that something quite different is at stake. In Jewish meditation on the story the question is asked "What was the bush that burned?" and an answer is proposed that perhaps the bush that burned like this was Israel, the people, which in all its sufferings was not consumed. That immediately links the incident to the whole life experience of Moses and suggests that the bush and the other material items that are mentioned, like the shoes, are an analogy. It suggests that the story is really talking about human affairs and an overwhelming revelation to Moses about the manner and focus of God's concern and intervention in human affairs. In this case, it is a story about the kind of thing that may happen to any of us at any time if we "take our shoes off," that is, if we approach events in our lives and in history with a sense of reverence, ready to see that the whole world is the place of God. If this is so, the message contained in the revelation is certainly not that there is a God, because that is assumed in the story, but rather that God is immensely and powerfully compassionate, that human suffering does not escape his attention and that he acts in and through human sensitivity and creativity.

This story of the burning bush interprets the deliverance of the Hebrews from Egypt for us by seeing the liberation of these oppressed people from political, economic and social domination as an exercise of the compassion of God who calls them to be his people in freedom and dignity and responsibility. Moreover, this story and others that follow it in the biblical text interpret that exodus from the oppression in Egypt in a way that makes it the prototype of saving actions in which God shows himself (is revealed) as powerfully compassionate. This story, therefore, of the burning bush and of exodus, sets a kind of pattern for the language and imagery with which not only Jews but Christians also interpret and hand on to future generations their further experiences of God revealing himself.

The burning bush of Christians is the resurrection of Jesus.

This will be discussed at length in Part II of this book. At this point it is important to notice only that the experience of the early followers of Jesus which defied all attempts at description or definition is the foundation of all Christian faith in the powerful compassion of God as made immediately present in our lives in the person of Jesus of Nazareth. Moreover, this foundation event not only established the grounds of Christian faith once long ago in the beginning, but is presented by the teaching of the Church as something which all Christian believers at all times in history in some way share. Here also, the point of the stories of resurrection appearances to various disciples does not seem to be that something so extraordinary happened that we should not expect to experience anything at all like it. Rather the point seems to be that the stories about the resurrection set up a prototype or a model by which we are to learn to recognize God revealing himself in Jesus of Nazareth to us in the experiences of our lives and of the history of our people.

Revelation, then, the transforming of our awareness, our understanding, our ability to perceive and interpret reality, is something that is open at all times to all of us. But that raises the question as to how the Christian revelation, seen as a quite particular body of teachings, relates to this continuing, universal revelation. Both Jews and Christians have long wrestled with this, and the basic answer they gave was that there is only one God who reveals himself and that therefore the basic content of revelation is always the same, namely the powerful compassion and ultimate claims of that God for human persons and societies. In the traditions of Israel there is the central conviction of a covenant or alliance made by God with his people Israel. In that covenant God reveals himself and his intentions in history. This is based upon the stories of Abraham and Moses and is very specific. Alongside this understanding, however, is the story of the covenant of Noah, the covenant of the rainbow made with all peoples, in which God also reveals himself as the Lord and Savior of all peoples without any of the specific content of the Mosaic covenant. The question then arises concerning the relationship of the two covenants and the two revelations. The answer given is that there is really only one covenant and one God revealing himself but that different peoples at different times share in this revelation more or less intimately and explicitly according to their calling.

The early Christian community was faced most urgently with the question of the relationship between God's self-revelation in Jesus of Nazareth which they had received and the revelation of the Mosaic covenant within which the life and teaching of Jesus himself was set. The Christian answer was essentially the same as the Hebrew answer had been; there is only one God revealing himself, and just as he had revealed himself in various ways in the past through the prophets, so now he had revealed himself more intimately through his own Son (Heb. 1:1–2).

This leads very quickly to another question concerning who is entitled to interpret God's revelation, and beyond this to the more difficult question of the relationship between the revelation itself and its particular formulation in the words of Scripture, creedal confessions of the churches, liturgical and conciliar texts and so forth. This is a contemporary question which troubles people frequently, but it arose already in the ancient Church. In the earliest centuries the Christian Gnostics claimed to have a special and privileged knowledge of the inner or hidden meaning of the Gospels. In other words they claimed that they had access to God's self-revelation in Jesus Christ that bypassed the testimony of the Church. The answer of the Church, as given by Irenaeus and other Church Fathers, is that the true revelation (the true Gospel, the true message of Jesus Christ) has been handed down through the generations in the whole Church and nothing has been kept back. Clearly, God's self-revelation is never exhausted by the formulations in words which the Church hands down, but these formulations are the one basic and reliable interpretation in words that we have.

Following the attacks of the Gnostics, the Montanist movement troubled and confused believing Christians. The Montanists claimed to have received new revelations which would add to or change the Christian Gospel as it was understood from the beginning. Of course, people were confused, as they are today when there are claims of new revelation, whether inside or outside the Church. In the struggle against the confusion caused by the Montanists, who demanded much stricter asceticism and observances than the churches had traditionally taught, the Church established the principle of a distinction between "public" and "private" revelation. "Public" revelation is that self-revelation of God in Jesus Christ which was received in the beginning by the apostles and the community that formed around them (the apostolic community) and which was handed on by them to future generations. In time this came to be called by the rather quaint name of "the deposit of faith." This does not refer to a particular document nor even to a clearly defined corpus or collection of documents; it includes whatever testimonies can be traced back to the apostolic community. "Private" revelations would include such events as the visions of mystics and the messages of Lourdes or Fatima. These are never added to "the deposit of faith," the "public" revelation that is handed on by the Church, but they are not necessarily condemned as false. If they are in keeping with the Gospel and the traditional faith of the Church and if they seem helpful in present circumstances and tend to build up Christian faith and spirituality, then the Church may even officially establish feastdays or encourage devotional practices based upon these "private" revelations. In other words, they are not necessarily private in the ordinary sense of the word but only in the technical sense that they are not to be considered part of "the deposit of faith."

Since the medieval era the Church has struggled with another question about revelation, namely the relation between faith and reason. This issue also is still very much alive today. Faith is, by definition, the assent of the mind to God revealing himself. This raises the question whether there is anything at stake here other than human reason wrestling, as it always does, with data of experience presented to it in order to grasp, interpret and integrate new knowledge. Clearly, the Church's understanding from the beginning is that the response of faith is more than the usual wrestling of the mind with evidence, because faith is not so much a matter of our minds grasping something as it is a matter of our minds allowing themselves to be grasped by something. The "something" here is the mystery of God which eludes our mastery because we really have no categories or language in which to contain it, but which invites us nevertheless into a new depth dimension of knowledge if we allow that mystery to master us. Because we are in the realm of things which it is not in the nature of the human mind to know, the rather quaint claim has been made in Christian teaching that by revelation God "shares with us his self-knowledge."

In fact, however, we do speak about the content of revelation. This whole book is about it. The way we are able to speak about it is in a language of poetry that makes hints and suggestions, a language of analogy in which we tell stories and experiences which cumulatively build up expectations and assurances that go far beyond what we can see and test. This is the language of much of Scripture, most of the texts of the liturgy, a good deal of the writings of the Church Fathers, all the writings of the mystics and the bulk of sermons and books on the Christian life. Yet Christians have not been content with this sort of language. They have yearned for expressions that are more explicit and more systematic. The effort to state the content of revelation in a more explicit and more systematic way is theology. The official formulations of councils and Popes are often made in the language of theology. These formulations claim to give a certain definition to the content of revelation.

Certainly, in the language of theology there is always an intensive use of human reasoning. There is always an attempt to understand the content of revelation. In answer to the question about the role of human reasoning in the interplay between God's revelation and the human person's faith, Catholic teaching has insisted that reason has a positive role to play. Reason must in the first place test the grounds of credibility. Not everything that claims to be a revelation of God is such. That was part of the issue with the Montanists. Not everyone who claims to bring a revelation from God is trustworthy. There have been many false prophets. Therefore, being perfectly docile to God revealing himself necessarily also means being intelligently critical of claims to present God's revelation. In the past, fundamental theology and apologetics were sometimes taught very widely and intensively. This was a way to share with Catholics the critical scrutiny of sources and claims that had already been conducted on their behalf, so that they could be strengthened by other people's learning and wisdom. However, there is no way to relieve the individual from the personal task of assessing the grounds of credibility. Most of us do not do this in a formal or self-conscious way, but we do it quietly nevertheless. We decide whom it is reasonable to believe and why and under what conditions it is reasonable to believe.

This is really the preliminary task in which reason is in quest of a faith. Much contemporary writing on religious topics is concerned with this preliminary task—writing on the nature of religious language, on the possibility of religious certitude, on the relation between history and faith claims, and so forth. The second task of reason in the response of faith is to seek for understanding within the assent of faith to God revealing himself when that assent has already been made. This concern and the phrase "faith seeking understanding" were emphasized and discussed particularly by Anselm of Canterbury in the eleventh century. Anselm's writings sometimes give the impression that he thought we could prove everything in Christian faith by reason, including the Divine Trinity. But perhaps his position could be stated like this: It is possible to attain a reasonable and fully integrated understanding within the Christian faith, because truth is one and the believer need not be afraid to ask questions and to use "secular" knowledge.

This, indeed, is what Albert the Great and his famous student, Thomas Aquinas, did in the thirteenth century. Thomas explicitly spoke of two sources for "sacred doctrine" (that is, theology as we know it). These were the truths of revelation and the truths of reason. There could not ultimately be a conflict between them. Apparent conflicts were due to incomplete or incorrect knowledge or understanding. However, the truths of revelation were precisely those which had not come from human reasoning in the first place but from the special gift of God. For Thomas that included two kinds of revelations: truths that we could have come to by reason, but which on account of our ignorance or distorted vision God was gracious enough to offer us in special revelatory events, and truths which by their nature we could not possibly ever have known by reason.

The principle that there could not ultimately be a conflict between the truths of revelation and the truths of reason came into play again with the advent of modern science, for instance in relation to astronomy and the structure of the universe (featured in the famous Galileo case) and much later in relation to evolutionary theories about the species of living organisms. In relation to the natural sciences the process of discerning the right interaction between faith and reason has been a stormy one. Sometimes loyally minded churchmen have wanted to close off research and reflection too soon. It seemed to them that certain scientific theories being proposed were so flagrantly and irredeemably in conflict with the faith that they could not be tolerated. In many such instances the calm conviction that there cannot ultimately be a conflict did in the end triumph. If there cannot ultimately be a conflict, then further scholarly investigation of the matter cannot endanger the faith.

In modern religious thought, the question of faith and reason has been raised in a different way. There have been many attempts to reduce religion to philosophy by stripping it of its particulars (which are known and appreciated by insiders only) and reducing everything to universal categories (which can be understood and agreed upon by all). The work of Hegel is important in this connection. It has influenced Protestant theology very deeply and has been a challenge to Catholic theology. In the nineteenth and twentieth centuries the official teaching voice of the Church, vested in the Holy See, has constantly protested against any position that seemed to reduce religious faith to philosophy. Some of these protests are turning out to be based upon misunderstandings, as with some who were called Modernists, but the basic concern is a very important one, namely that we know that God does show himself and his purposes in history to us in ways that are beyond the reach of our unaided reason.

Related Material

More detailed information about the early Christian heresies and controversies mentioned in this and the following chapters is available in very readable form in Early Christian Doctrines *by J. N. D. Kelly (Harper & Row).*

A very comprehensive but concise and readable account of the many ways Christians have understood and spoken about revelation is available in Revelation Theology *by Avery Dulles (Herder/ Seabury). This book is almost entirely concerned with revelation the-*

ology since the Protestant Reformation of the sixteenth century as it has been developed by particular authors in the various Christian denominations. Theology of Revelation *by Rene Latourelle (Mercier Press) devotes about 170 pages to pre-Reformation authors and is entirely concerned with Catholic authors in the post-Reformation period. Both these books give concise accounts of the official Catholic Church teachings of the Council of Trent and the Second Vatican Council.*

Many Christians have found helpful insights of a far-reaching personal kind into the meaning of revelation (and of faith which is the obverse side of revelation) in the section entitled "Revelation" in God in Search of Man *by the Jewish author A. J. Heschel (Harper & Row).*

2

Creation in God's Image

The doctrine of creation becomes clearer when we ask ourselves what question this doctrine is supposed to answer. It may seem as though it answers the question about how everything in the world began in the first place. This, however, is not the concern either of the biblical stories or of the Christian doctrines that have been formulated on the basis of the biblical stories. In fact, how everything began is not a religious or spiritual question because it has no bearing on how to live a life that is open to God in faith, hope and charity. It is rather a question for scientific and philosophical speculation because it does have a bearing on technological projections and experiments, and it does influence the ways in which history and human cultures are observed and analyzed.

When religion (or myth) speaks of creation, the underlying question is concerned with the meaning of human life. The question arises out of human experience, and apparently out of the experience of finitude and contingency. We are finite in the sense that we are born at a particular place and time and will surely die one day, and in the sense that we are limited in our knowledge, our power to act, our influence and our whole being. We are contingent because we might so easily not have been at all if our parents had not come together, if the time had not been right, if we had not been brought to live birth, if we had not survived. We are contingent because day by day we depend on clean air, unpolluted water, food, firm ground beneath us, sheltering roofs above us, protective clothing about us and so much more. In other words, we simply cannot take our own existence for granted, and we are prompted to ask why we exist and what is the meaning of our lives.

In response to this question the Bible tells us several stories out of the treasury of folklore of ancient Israel. These stories are couched in the language of myth. They speak in concrete images about beginnings and causes of a vast cosmic history. They speak in this way because they are telling of matters that lie beyond the boundaries of precise, appropriate and masterful language. They must speak in the language of poetic imagery and suggestion, in the language of analogy. Two of these stories, the basic ones, are found in the first two chapters of Genesis, the book that is placed at the very beginning of our Bible as we have it today. The older of the two stories is the one given in Chapter 2. This story tells that when "the Lord God" made earth and heaven, nothing grew because there was no rain and no tiller of the soil, though the land seems to have rested precariously on water that would break through and flood everything sometimes. But God made a person (adam) out of earth (adamah) and breathed life into him. God also made a garden on a fertile, delightful plain "to the east," full of fruit-bearing trees and watered by a river in four streams. Here he put the person as caretaker of the garden, with instructions that he might eat any of the fruit except that of the tree of "the knowledge of good and evil" which would bring him death. God made animals and birds and presented them to the person; he in turn named them but found no companionship in them, so God drew from the person's side a woman and in her the person was finally able to recognize one like himself with whom he had partnership and companionship.

This splendid story, rich in symbolism and allusions, has given food for thought and prayer to Hebrews and Christians for thousands of years. When one enjoys it and reflects on it simply as a story, several points emerge in answer to the questions why we exist and what is the meaning of our lives. First of all, life is a gift, and the image of the garden in the valley of delight suggests that it is a good gift, an abundant gift, the gift of one who takes pleasure in bestowing happiness. At the same time the gift of life is not an idle gift. It is also a task for the receiver, because the person is placed in the garden as caretaker to till it. Moreover, it is a story of contentment and freedom, but of freedom with limits. This person is given a freedom to enjoy the fruits of the garden, but the freedom is "situated" within the conditions that are healthful and give life. Freedom is not to be pressed beyond those boundaries or it will lead to death. There are therefore commands attached to this human existence which is so far beyond the life of the animals in the story. The dignity and freedom of human life carry a moral exigence. The dignity and freedom also call for companionship, partnership, community, interpersonal relationships of like with like, represented by the man and the woman.

In the minds of Hebrews and Christians this story is set beside a later one which our Bible, however, gives in Chapter 1 of Genesis. This story, which in the Hebrew lends itself beautifully to being chanted aloud, is in fact a series of seven tableaux in which an ordered, harmonious, habitable universe is brought out of apparent chaos by God's command. All that is brought forth is given its proper place—light and darkness, the waters and the sky-vaulted air space, the seas and the dry land, the fruits and the seeds in their appropriate plants, the sun, moon and stars, the birds of the air and the fish of the various waters, animals of all sorts, and human persons male and female to rule over all living beings and take possession of this ordered universe. There are six tableaux in which God accomplishes all these things and sees that they are good, that they are finally very good, and there is a seventh tableau in which God is shown as resting and contemplating his work and blessing the seventh day of the week that we might likewise enjoy it as a day of rest and contemplation.

Central to this second story is the human person male and female in the likeness of God. It is this human person for whose use and enjoyment and contemplation all else is ordered. Persons do not exist for these things, but all things exist for persons. Things are not to rule over persons but persons over things. That appears to leave unanswered the original question as to why we exist and what is the meaning of our lives in the context of this second story. Further reflection, however, suggests that the tableau of the seventh day on which God rests and contemplates so that we who are in the image of God may learn to do the same tells us that our existence is oriented to God. The meaning of our lives is discovered when the things of creation do not dominate us but when we use the good gifts of creation in a freedom that draws our attention on beyond the creatures to the Creator.

Because Hebrew and Christian prayer and reflection have placed these two creation stories side by side and have added to them further imagery taken, for instance, from the psalms, a rather coherent answer emerges to the two questions about our existence. We exist because God wills it, because God calls us into existence and sustains us in existence with the many and wonderful gifts of his creation, and because God intends above all that we be happy in being like him, with him and for him. Moreover, according to these stories we are not left guessing as to how we are to do this. God shares with us the wisdom or the principles of harmony by which he governs the universe and holds all things in place. He tells us the boundaries that establish our place in creation and warns us of that which is beyond the boundaries and can only lead to death. This understanding is powerfully expressed, for instance, in Psalm 19: there is a harmony in the movement of the sun through the heavens and there is a parallel harmony in the commandments of God that govern human lives. The same point is made with slightly different imagery in Psalm 24.

Christians say more than this, however. In the prologue to the Gospel according to John, Jesus is identified with the divine word by which all things came to be in the creation. He is also identified with the life and the light of the world. In the Letter of Paul to the Colossians Jesus is described as the image of the invisible God, the prince of creation through whom and for whom all things are created and in whom all things are held together (Col. 1:15–18). This is another way of saying that we understand what the creation stories mean from our experience of Jesus. In him we see the image of God, his own image in which he made human persons. In him we see the harmony established by God's law which holds all things in place or in balance. In him we see the freedom of a man who is not dominated by the things of creation but who uses all things in the context of his focus toward the transcendent God, and therefore completes humanly the harmony and purpose of creation by drawing all things into his praise of God. For Christians, therefore, Jesus is not only the redeemer from sin (which is discussed in Part II of this book) but he is seen as the very pattern of creation, the fullness of the human person in the image of God, the key to the questions concerning why we exist and what is the meaning of our lives.

In the course of the centuries Christians could not be content simply to repeat and to hand on the biblical stories and images. They were forced to ask many times and under many different circumstances what these stories meant in terms of life among the Gentiles, in terms of the Greek thought world, in terms of Christian attitudes and behavior in changing social, political and cultural settings, in terms of changing economies and so forth. Moreover, many times the Christian doctrine of creation was challenged in some far-reaching way.

In the second century of Christian history the Gnostic movement responded to the experience of evil in the world (which Christians answered as told in the following chapter) in a strange way that has proved to be a recurring temptation in subsequent history. They taught that the world of our experience really has two different origins or sources which are opposed to each other and cause the tension and confusion in human lives. Our souls or spirits come from a good creation by a power of light and goodness and spirit, or they are an exiled part of light and spirit. Our bodies, they maintained, like all material things are the creation of an evil power, a force of darkness and matter. This doctrine appeared in many forms. It was probably not originally a Christian error but a way of looking at reality that arose quite outside the Christian community. However, it came to be quite attractive and seductive to many Christians because it seemed to give such easy and straightforward answers to many things. In fact it came back to haunt Christians in the fourth century in the teachings of the Manichaeans and in the twelfth century in the doctrines of the Cathari (often referred to as Albigensians), and it has had certain further echoes in the practical teachings of Jansenism since the seventeenth century and in a modern tendency to individualize Christian spirituality and isolate it from the practical affairs of the world.

From the second century onward, beginning with the writings of the Church Father Irenaeus, there has been a very strong Christian reaction to this whole line of thought. Almost instinctively Christians, like Jews, react against any suggestion that there could be two Gods, or even that there could be another great force not subject to God but antithetical to him. This is why Christian teaching has come to insist that God has created and does create "out of nothing," although these words are not found in the biblical accounts and do not appear in a major creed until the profession of faith of the Fourth Lateran Council in 1215. It is also the reason for which the creeds composed since the time of the Council of Nicea in 325 have spoken of God as Creator of "all things visible and invisible."

This passionate concern over the unity of God (whom, however, Christians see as triune, as will be discussed in Part IV of this book) is more than a theoretical issue of orthodoxy or true faith for Christians. Our whole Christian life and manner of response depends on the unity of God. Because God is the whole horizon of reality, the sole source of our existence and that of all other things and forces, he therefore has an ultimate and all-embracing claim on us, clearly our whole being, our attitudes and values, our doings and relationships, what we are and what we become, what we love and what we avoid must be brought to focus on God as the goal and purpose of our lives if those lives are to have coherent meaning. In the Gnostic understanding this is not so. The spirit of the human person must return to the light from which it came, but this does not involve the body in its relationships, its activities and experiences in the world; therefore there is a certain ambiguity and a certain denial of much of the real world of our experience in a person's turning to God or a person's quest for the meaning of life under the inspiration and guidance of Gnostic teaching.

Moreover, in the Christian understanding, because all that is in heaven and earth, all that is visible and invisible is the creation of the one good and all-powerful God, we can be soberly optimistic in our effort to make all things serve rather than master us in our service of God. We can expect to discover the intrinsic harmony of God's good creation in all aspects of nature, and of human affairs (in spite of sin which will be discussed in the following chapter, and because of God's healing and restoring grace which will be discussed in Part III of this book). In the Gnostic view this is not so. Nothing material can serve the soul's journey back to the light. There is irreconcilable tension and opposition not only between soul and body, spiritual life and sexuality, care for bodily needs and so forth, but also between an earnest quest for one's personal goal and concern with social, economic and political affairs of the world in which one might serve the needs of others in maintaining or bettering the conditions in which they must live their lives. In a properly Christian perspective, honest work and effort in the world, including political, economic, social and cultural activities, are an exercise of the love of God which is never separable from the love of other people, and in some sense from the love of all God's good creation. Therefore even intense involvement in public affairs is not incompatible with a single-minded pursuit of a person's ultimate goal and meaning in life which is God. It only comes in conflict with this pursuit if the involvement in public affairs is selfish, oppressive of others, arrogant, or in some way in rebellion against God. Likewise, in a properly Christian perspective the most complete and absorbing and intense realization of human sexuality in marital fidelity is not incompatible with the total and passionate orientation of one's life to God as its goal and meaning. It is rather the exploitation or bullying or manipulation or defrauding of another person that is in truth incompatible with the turning of one's life to God.

The preceding paragraph should be enough to demonstrate that the distortions consequent upon the assertion that there are two Gods continue in many ways to haunt us. Catholic people today are still often inclined to think that the quest for God in one's life must be a turning away from other people, even from their needs. In particular, many Catholics think that religion and politics must be forever quite different realms with quite different values and criteria. More careful reflection suggests that this is a kind of dualism. It suggests that political affairs form a realm in which God does not and cannot rule, a realm which is intractable to God's power and apparently subject to an alien and oppositional power. In the same way, many Catholics still appear to think that enjoyable friendship and fellowship with others is a distraction from God and that sexual relationships in themselves point away from God completely though they might be somewhat redeemed by the struggle to raise a godly family. Such attitudes all seem to be a subtle denial of the unity and omnipotence of God who is the Creator of all things and who makes the human person and human society in his own image.

Another and related challenge to the doctrine of creation that dates back to the second century but has had echoes through the ages is that of the Marcionites who saw an opposition between an angry vengeful God of justice of the Hebrew Scriptures (the Old Testament) and a loving forgiving God introduced to us by Jesus in the New Testament. Those who defended Christian orthodoxy then and since have usually understood the Marcionites to claim that there really were two different Gods, one of the order of creation who judged by strict law and justice and was therefore an avenger and punisher, and one of the order of redeeming grace who judged by compassion and was therefore a pardoner and rescuer. One consequence of the dichotomy was that the whole testimony of the Hebrew Scriptures, including the creation accounts described at the beginning of this chapter, became irrelevant according to the Marcionites for a Christian understanding of the goal and meaning of life. But it is perhaps in its more subtle forms that the Marcionite teaching has continued to be a threat to Christian faith and understanding down to our own times.

One of these forms is that which asserts not two different Gods but two wholly different conceptions of God. Thus, Jews saw God as just and vengeful, a warrior and conqueror, while Christians saw God as loving and merciful, a father and protector. This is an intolerable distinction. In the first place it is untrue. Secondly, it gives a misleading picture not only of the Jewish but also of the Christian understanding of God. It does not do justice to the exigence of God revealed to us in Jesus. The merciful Father of Jesus does claim ultimate and total allegiance even at the cost of tragedy and suffering and death, and the story of Jesus himself shows this. The story of Jesus, in fact, asks us to acknowledge that the overwhelming love of God for us is shown in God's far-reaching claims on us and not in spite of them.

Yet another challenge to the doctrine of creation has come many times through the ages from different forms of pantheism. Pantheism views God and the world (including human persons) as one being; the world and all that is in it is not a creation of finite beings set over against God, but is an emanation or self-expression of God. The Church in its official responses has been very firm in opposing such thinking, beginning with later followers of the third-century Church Father, Origen, and the followers of a Spanish Manichaean of the fourth century, Priscillian. There are good reasons for this opposition to pantheism in all its forms. Pantheism tends to justify whatever is in fact happening in the world, while Christian faith calls for a prophetic scrutiny of what is happening in order to discern what is good and what is sinful, which structures and values and expectations are redemptive and which are blocking God's redemptive grace. Moreover, if everything is an expression or emanation of God, there is likely to be less respect for individual human persons, particularly for the poor and the forgotten or unfortunate. Christian faith, on the other hand, is particularly concerned to defend the dignity and the rights of the poorest and the most despised. Prayer is also seen very differently according to a pantheistic and according to a Christian creation faith.

Perhaps the most interesting issue that has arisen over the doctrine of creation is that of the relation between science and revelation in our understanding of the universe and its history. The question was raised in the sixteenth century over the issue of the Copernican model of the universe in which our earth was no longer seen as the center. But this question was intensified in the nineteenth and twentieth centuries over the issue of evolutionary views of the living species, including the human. It seemed to many believers that evolutionary theories were in clear contradiction to the revealed truth as given to us in the Bible and in the traditional teachings of the Church. At first it seemed to be so because in the nineteenth and early twentieth century most Christians, including theologians and members of the hierarchy, took the Genesis creation stories rather literally, unaware of the literary genre intended by the original authors of those stories. Gradually biblical scholarship cleared up this misunderstanding, in spite of much resistance and anguish.

Later, the religious objections to theories of evolution became more subtle. They were concerned with the value and dignity given to the human person, and they feared that a view of human persons which put them in continuity with sub human ancestors would also undermine the understanding of the human soul as spiritual, individually created and unconditionally precious to God. An encyclical letter of Pope Pius XII, *Humani generis*, written in 1950, settled the matter by saying that Christian doctrine leaves the question of evolution wide open but insists on three points: the individual creation of each human soul, the authority of revelation in speaking to us of the source of our being, and the unity of the human race.

These three points are immediately relevant to contemporary issues. It is because of the belief in the individual creation of the human soul and the consequent dignity and unconditional worth of each person that the Catholic Church takes such an uncompromising stand on abortion, on euthanasia and suicide, on the rights of retarded and "unwanted" persons, and on the social justice claims of starving and oppressed populations.

These can never be seen as waste on the margins of the evolutionary process. It is because we acknowledge the authority of revelation in speaking to us of the source of our being that we cannot accept uncritically philosophical or psychological theories of human personality and personality development, but must subject them to serious scrutiny as to whether they are consonant with the godward focus intrinsic to the human person as seen by the doctrine of creation. It is because of the insistence on the unity of the human race as God's creation that all racial discrimination and exclusion appears as ultimately incompatible with Christian faith.

These points being clarified, it has become evident during the last few decades that an evolutionary view of the universe and of the human situation may in fact be a more helpful context for the doctrine of creation than a static view. Certainly the Genesis stories speak of the human person as a maker like God, as one who is destined to bring order, to name, to "found" a habitable world. They do not speak of the world as finished. It is equally sure that John and Paul in the New Testament, seeing Jesus as the focus and center of creation, present creation as something in the present, something continuing through time and continuing in the midst of the struggle with sin and destruction. In our times, Pierre Teilhard de Chardin, the great Jesuit scientist, developed a vast and prayerful vision of the whole creation as it comes from God and returns to God through Christ, all based upon a very comprehensive evolutionary perspective.

Since the time of Teilhard de Chardin's posthumous publications, it has become increasingly clear that in human affairs evolution has become a conscious and responsible human activity. The world is so sharply divided into the relatively rich and the quite desperately poor, not because at some far distant past time God decreed it so and that is the way things have continued under his providence in the world, but rather because the resources God continually creates for the benefit of us all are continually being appropriated by the more powerful to the exclusion of all the others. The orthodox Catholic doctrine calls upon us to see the great questions of social justice and social structuring not in terms of a static situation created by God at the beginning, but in terms of a continuing interaction of God's bountiful creativity with human freedoms in all their selfishness, sinfulness and limitations. This suggests that the doctrine of creation does not simply justify or guarantee the present order of things as God's will. Rather this doctrine offers us a radical critique of the present order of things by the light of a vision of how it is intended in God's good creation.

Related Material

Besides the general sources already mentioned, especially Early Christian Doctrines *by J. N. D. Kelly, readers may find the following helpful.* God's World in the Making *by Piet Schoonenberg (Seabury) and* Covenant and Creation, *also by Schoonenberg (Notre Dame Press), contain a set of essays concerned with several modern questions in the area of creation theology.* Man Before God: Toward a Theology of Man *by Juan Alfaro et al., compiled at the Canisianum in Innsbruck (Kenedy), has a number of essays on spirit and matter, freedom and community, which are concerned with creation theology. A detailed historical account of the development of the doctrine of creation is available in* Creation and Providence *by Leo Scheffczyk (Herder).*

3

Sin and Sinfulness

The doctrine of creation alone does not give a satisfactory account of the world as we know it. In fact, in the context of the doctrine of creation without further qualification, faith in Jesus Christ does not make sense. At the heart of Christian faith stands the cross of Jesus who died to save us from sin and sinfulness and their consequences. To accept the Christian message, acknowledge Jesus as one's Savior and become a follower of Jesus is only possible if one recognizes sin in the world. It means acknowledging that the world as we know it is not simply God's good creation but a distortion of that creation by sin. It means, further, acknowledging one's own sinfulness, seeing oneself not only as God's good creation but as a sinner in whom the creative purpose of God (which ought to integrate and make total sense of life) is to some extent warped and frustrated (causing a certain disintegration and loss of focus).

The cross of Jesus is for Christians a startling and even blinding revelation of sin in the world, as well as the revealing and transforming moment of God's redeeming love. When Christians confront the crucified Jesus with their creation faith, they cannot but ask the question: "What went wrong?" Yet Christians were not the first to ask that question. Long before the time of Jesus, Israel had asked that question. Indeed anyone who looks at the world as it is, looks at it unflinchingly and sees what is really there, must ask that same question, "What went wrong?"

Again, Israel answered its own question with stories. Before looking at the Genesis story of sin and the fall, it is necessary to recall a story that is at the foundation of Jewish and Christian consciousness, and is taken for granted in the biblical texts, but which never found its way into the canon of Scripture. This is the story of an angelic creation part of which fell away from the harmony with God. The story envisages an earlier phase, before the creation of the world we know. God is shown as calling into existence great and powerful and very beautiful beings, intelligent and free. They are called into being to find their happiness in the praise of God, and most in fact respond and realize the purpose of their creation. Some, however, look rather at themselves in admiration, making themselves the object of their existence. The ancient legends tell of a great battle in heaven in which the rebel angel hosts attack in the form of a great metal dragon under the leadership of a mighty one whom Christians have come to name Lucifer, the light-bearer. Heaven, as the place of God and the realm of harmony, truth and beauty, is also defended by an angel host under the leadership of one named Michael, or "Who shall be like to God?" The Book of Revelation in the New Testament refers to this story among others.

In this ancient story, Lucifer and his angels are thrust down into a place of their own, and the peace of the heavenly realm of the angelic creation is restored. But the spirit of rebellion and self-aggrandizement is not extinct. The rebel host bide their time. The creation of the world that we know is set between the heavenly realm and the hell of the rebel angels whose existence is torment because they seek their meaning and fulfillment in themselves and are therefore doomed to utter frustration. Our world is seen as poised between the two, because the human persons in it are intelligent and free with a freedom that is not yet finally committed to God or self, to the heavenly realm or to the hell of the fallen angels. Moreover, our world is seen as caught in a dynamic interplay of the two. Jewish and Christian thought sees the human community and individual human beings as called, inspired, helped and guarded not by God alone but by the presence and powerful intervention of angels, messengers from the heavenly realm, servants and helpers of God. This is how angels come to play a part in the Bible and in Christian fantasy, piety and doctrine. On the other hand, Jewish and Christian thought has seen human beings and the structure of society and even the physical universe as subjected to a certain domination by the evil forces of the lower world that draws all to destruction and frustration away from God. Lucifer and his host, also known as the devil and his angels, are understood to have a mysterious hold over the world and human affairs. Life in our world is seen, therefore, as a struggle between forces that are greater than we are. This is how Satan, the tempter, or the devil comes to play so large a role in Scripture and in Christian folklore and doctrine.

It may be worthwhile to reflect on the meaning of this story of the creation, fall and battle of the angels before considering the Genesis story of the fall of Adam and Eve. First of all, this story is part of the ancient Hebrews' answer to the question about what went wrong in God's good creation. Secondly, it clearly means to tell us that what went wrong is something bigger than any of us is able to tackle, and even bigger than all of us together are able to overcome. The story certainly also means to tell us that we are intimately, inescapably and tragically affected by this problem of rebellion against God that is so much bigger than we are. Beyond this, the story helps to explain human sin and sinfulness. It tries to explain the easy surrender of Adam and Eve to the spirit of rebellion and self-aggrandizement in spite of their enjoyment of the close friendship of God.

In other words, the story seems to be an effort to take the origin of evil in human affairs and in the world one step further back behind any human failure. The ancient storytellers surely did this because that is how the situation looked to them; they found themselves unable to assign the whole blame to human beings because the damage seemed to go so far beyond what human beings might have caused. Yet they certainly did not want to assign the blame to God for a creation that was warped. Nor did they want to give in to any dualism that would see the cause of evil as another great power quite independent of God in its origin and operation. They could not see the problem that lay beyond the human. It could not be revealed to them in terms other than those of their own experience and it could not be expressed in terms other than those of their own language and culture. They really "wrote large" the basic human dilemma, namely that freedom cannot exist without risk. Intelligent creatures are free to fulfill their destiny out of their inner spontaneity with genuine love. This leads to a deep communion of experience with others and with God. But it necessarily carries the risk that that freedom might be used so as to frustrate the purpose of human existence and destroy human happiness.

The story which is given to us explicitly in Scripture is the one which begins in the third chapter of Genesis but has further echoes in the following chapters in the stories of Cain and Abel, the flood, the tower of Babel and so forth. The entry of the serpent (the ancient dragon which was not then without legs) into the garden in the valley of delight begins the biblical account of sin. The serpent tempts the companion and the companion tempts Adam. They are tempted to an act of explicit disobedience with the motivation that it will make them like God—not in the image or likeness of God that results from their worship of God and their total and willing dependence on God for their being and their destiny, but rather like gods, independent of God, asserting themselves in opposition to him.

The immediate results are depicted in the story. They become painfully aware of their nakedness, their vulnerability; they are embarrassed or afraid to be under scrutiny simply for what they are. They lose the experience of God's friendship and intimate presence with them not because of God's anger but because of their own fear which drives them into hiding. Before this their whole environment responded harmoniously to God's creative call which brought it into existence. It is now experienced as hostile and disrupted when they take over command as independent gods who determine good and evil. In fact, they discover that when they assert their independence from God they no longer master the creatures of the world but are dominated and enslaved by them. They discover this in the pain and suffering with which they maintain themselves in the world and which seems so senseless. When this is put in the mouth of God in the story it is not as a vindictive judgment against them but rather as an explanation of the way creation is structured and the consequences of thwarting its intrinsic focus toward God. If there is a verdict in the scene in which God confronts them, that verdict is rather in the promise that the power of the great tempter will be reduced so that they will not be helpless against him and that there shall be a redemption out of the exile from the presence of God and from the garden. This is in the divine proclamation that the serpent shall now crawl on its belly eating dust and that its head is to be crushed by the seed of the woman.

This is a magnificent story. It is not a story about something that happened long ago to other people who were not at all like us. It is rather a story about the whole human situation, about each of us and all of us, today as in other times. It is a story about the continuing present in which all of us live. It is a story that attempts to discern and to tell us what it is that is going wrong now and has been going wrong throughout the history of the human race, what it is that puts us out of focus with God and out of harmony with God's creation. It is a story that picks up the refrain from Lucifer: I will not serve; I will exist as a god in my own right. Human sin is seen collectively as the echo of Lucifer's refrain, the assertion of unconditioned freedom, absolute freedom, quite outside its proper situation within the order of creation and within the offer of the gracious and gratuitous friendship of God. Human sin is also seen as disobedience, failure to respond, to the creative summons and gracious invitation of God. The point of the story seems to be that such disobedience, such failure to respond causes the world of God's good creating to fall apart.

When the earliest Christian communities claimed that the death of Jesus was for our salvation from sin, the focus was not so much on the specific sinful acts that each individual to be saved might have committed, but rather on this sin of Adam, this general state of sin in the world by which the whole human situation is set awry. Paul, for instance, sees Jesus as a second Adam in whom the consequences of sin are overcome so that the whole world can be reintegrated in him as a new creation; the solidarity of the human race in the disruptive effects of sin is exchanged for a solidarity in grace in Jesus (Rom. 5:12–21). This theme of Jesus as the second Adam and the project of redemption as a far-reaching transformation of all the sinful structures, values and expectations of the world is so fundamental that it is taken up, for instance, by Irenaeus in the second century, by Augustine of Hippo in the early fifth century, by Thomas Aquinas with the idea of the "grace of headship" in Christ in the thirteenth century, by John Henry Newman in hymnody in the nineteenth century, and so forth.

According to the New Testament, and especially according to Paul, sin and sinfulness are revealed to us (or become recognizable) in two phases: the law of Moses given on Sinai and the death of Jesus by crucifixion on Calvary. What Paul says of the law of Moses is, in some sense, true of our experience of any law at any time: it identifies evil by the things it forbids and commands but it does not in itself make it any easier to do good. At best law maintains an uneasy truce, a minimal external order, by guaranteeing a certain degree of justice among competing persons and groups and by adding the motivation of fear of penalties to be applied to transgressors. But law, even the best law, does not give life or love or healing; it does not restore joy or hope or give meaning to life. Law holds human greed and anger and arrogance at bay; it does not transform them into the spirit of community and service by which alone human existence finds its true focus and integration. But the law, any law, always holds a risk. It is possible to mistake law-abiding behavior for goodness. It is possible to suppose that where there is law and order there is no sin. This is why the Christian revelation of sin in its true colors in the crucifixion of Jesus is so shattering. What we learn from the cross of Jesus is that we cannot put our ultimate trust in all those respectable structures of law and order on which we usually depend.

In the passion and death and resurrection of Jesus it is the one who is outside the law who is vindicated by God as the sinless one, and all that is ranged against him is convicted as sinful. But what is ranged against him is almost everything in the structures and values of the world by which we usually judge right and wrong. What we see in the crucified and risen Jesus is that sin is far more pervasive in our lives, in our attitudes and in our world than we would otherwise be able to realize. Moreover, sin is so pervasive in the human situation that we cannot withdraw from it by our own strength. God's good creation is distorted out of focus not only around us but within us. Only by a new and gracious outreach, a kind of new creation, in which God restores the integrating focus toward himself, can we escape from the pervasive sin and sinfulness of the world around and within us. This is the gift of God, utterly gratuitous, given in God's way and in God's good time, never at human command or under human control.

This is what Christians mean when they speak of original sin and grace. This was a preoccupation of the apostle Paul in the letters of the New Testament. He sees a certain tension in himself and in the early followers of Jesus to whom his letters are addressed. It is the tension between law and grace, between the exigence of God's call to repentance and reliance on God's initiative alone. Paul saw this in the continuing anxiety that some Christians had about the observance of the ritual commandments of the Mosaic code (the law of Moses). He also saw it in the tendency to create new ritual observances to replace the old (Jewish) ones. The same issue arose in the time of Augustine of Hippo in the early fifth century in relation to the followers of a monk named Pelagius. The Pelagian heresy, as it became identified, was not concerned with ritual so much as with a strict but self-reliant moral code. The Pelagians seem to have taught that the basic human freedom with which we are endowed in our creation is sufficient to make it possible for us to avoid sin totally and live good and holy lives. This ignores the Christian understanding that sin has quite distorted both our basic human freedom and the world in which we are called to live. The Pelagian position seems to say that we are able to redeem ourselves from sin, or at the least that we are able to steer our way through without personally committing sin. Later variations of this, which are sometimes called semi-Pelagian, suggest that while sinful we are able and required to program and conduct our own conversion.

St. Augustine responded to the Pelagians with so much passion that it is easy to misunderstand him. Nevertheless the

Catholic understanding of original sin and grace developed from his answers and was spelled out in some detail in the sixteenth century by the Council of Trent. The immediate occasion for this was the writing and preaching of Martin Luther. Luther saw many abuses in the Church of his time and thought that he saw both magical and semi-Pelagian suppositions at work. The Fathers of the Council of Trent, while themselves aware of the abuses and the confusion in understanding, were not ready to accept Luther's conclusions, so they set out the Catholic doctrine very explicitly.

The Catholic teaching is as follows. Original sin affects the whole human race and every person within it. It affects us from the very beginning of our existence. It affects us before we make any free choices, indeed before we have begun to develop the critical consciousness that makes free choices possible. To many people this has seemed an absurd proposition because it seemed so unfair. However, when we consider it concretely it becomes more or less self-evident. We do not form our thinking, our language, our values and expectations, our worldview, our understanding of life and its purpose, in isolation or in the abstract. We form them from what we learn in our relationships with other people and from our experiences and observations of the world in which we live. We are, or we become, what our relationships with others make us. This happens long before we are conscious enough, rational enough, critical enough, to begin to try to make ourselves what we think we ought to be. In other words, we are dependent in a very basic way on what others make us.

There is no such thing as beginning with a clean slate. This is so, for instance, in relation to selfishness and generosity, in relation to prejudices such as racial discrimination, in relation to patterns of competition and cooperation, in attitudes to material goods, status, reputation and so forth. In all such matters we must internalize the attitudes, values, and expectations of those around us long before we are in any position to reflect on those attitudes critically. In fact, it is always very difficult to arrive at a critical attitude to one's own values.

This much is simply common sense observation of society and people in their society. What Christian teaching adds to it is the assertion that this focus or orientation of our whole being which we cannot escape is necessarily a sinful one because of the "sin of Adam," because of the sinfulness of the world as we know it. It is a sinful one because the human community in which we are rooted, in which we have our origin, is out of focus and estranged from its end and purpose in God. This makes us individually in a rather literal sense originally sinful, that is, lacking the focus toward God. We do not simply begin our lives harmoniously focused toward God, valuing all things only insofar as they relate us back to God, comfortably and naturally respecting the freedom and rights and dignity of others and freely cooperating with them in perfect community. We do not have any experience of living like this before we begin to choose and deliberately misuse our personal freedom to do something destructive. Anyone who has raised children is painfully aware that this idyllic state of affairs does not exist among them. Even people with clear recollections of growing up among siblings know as much. If the actual state of affairs seems unfair, that may be because we have not thought enough about human freedom and about the extent of our responsibility for one another and especially for those who come after us. In any case, the fact of the matter is that we start out on our life's journey quite selfish and self-centered and flawed, and are immediately in need of redemption or rescue from our own sinfulness even before we have enough freedom to commit any personal sin.

The Catholic teaching further puts this into perspective by defining what this sinfulness is, explaining in what it consists. It is in the first place the loss of grace or friendship or intimacy with God. This assumes that such intimacy has already been offered to the human community as a gracious gift of God beyond what we might expect to be simply the pattern of creation. The teaching assumes that such grace has been offered and has been rejected by sin, by the posture of independence over against God that excludes such intimacy. The rejection of such intimacy with God by the human race taken corporately leaves each individual adrift, out of focus, lost, cut off from the goal that gives meaning to life. The loss of grace is not an isolated or one-dimensional experience in human life. It has consequences in all aspects of human existence. It has consequences in one's understanding and judgment, in one's ordering of priorities and affections, in the direction of one's will and in one's experience of contingency, limits and death.

Because of sin and sinful inclinations, we cannot assume that our reason will always be clear and unclouded. We must expect to find that self-interest, fear, anger, pride, prejudice and other factors may dim or distort our perceptions, our reasoning and our judgments. While the healing grace of God is held out to us in Christ and is given to anyone who responds to it in faith, this does not mean that the effects of sin and sinfulness are simply wiped out. The distortion of our seeing and thinking and judging is not suddenly wiped out by a first response of faith or by baptism into the Church. This distortion is only overcome by lifelong receptivity to the continuing graces of God. This, no doubt, is why we so often observe the obstinate persistence of racial prejudices or unrecognized continuance of social injustices in societies of believing and devout Christians.

Another consequence of sin which is not simply shed by faith or baptism is what is known as concupiscence or the inclination to sin. It implies that when the personal orientation has been turned away from God there is also a disorder in the person's affections, desires, priorities and ability to make decisive and firm choices and commitments. It is our common experience, even after an initial conversion to Christ and even after baptism, that our many wants and urges and desires are not in harmony, nor under the control of our will in its deliberate choices. It is the struggle of a lifetime to open oneself sufficiently to the grace of God that God may gradually refocus one's whole being toward himself so that all aspects of it may be drawn into that focus and may therefore fall back into place in an harmonious personal existence.

Perhaps the most significant aspect of this is the dimension of community with others. It is not only the inner coherence of each person that falls apart due to sin and sinfulness. It is also the coherence of the human race and of all our relationships with one another that is disrupted. The unwillingness to be dependent on God is most dramatically expressed in unwillingness to be interdependent with other people. The unwillingness to be for God or to serve God becomes concrete in the refusal to be for others or at their service. The story of sin in Genesis moves from the eating of the fruit in the garden to the fratricide of Abel by Cain and from there to innumerable treacheries, cruelties, injustices and injuries. The story expresses well the common human experience of the other person as threat rather than promise, rival rather than friend, constraint rather than freedom. All this too is an aspect of sinfulness, a consequence of the condition that we call original sin. This too points to the need of redemption or rescue by grace. True community, true cooperation and friendship and self-giving love are gifts of grace and not the outcome of unaided human efforts.

The foregoing derives its urgency and poignancy from the fact that we exist in the world in a very vulnerable way. We are conditioned and limited in time and space and in the pattern of relationships to other people and to the material world. Most of all we know we are mortal, that we shall surely die one day and that we can be killed any day. Mortality sums up with particular sharpness all our vulnerability. Mortality as we know it is a cause of fear that is particularly liable to distort our perceptions, reasoning and judgment. It is apt also to throw our choices and commitments out of focus, and to make our relationships with other people inauthentic. There is the fear of death itself, and there is also the fear of many losses associated with death. There is the fear of pain and suffering, of loss of property, of loss of respect and control and freedom of action. There is the fear of dependence on others and the fear of the unknown.

Catholic doctrine associates death and all its attendant fears and distortions as we experience them with original sin. It insists that death as we know it is not in the plan of God's good creation. Moreover, it points to the death and resurrection of Jesus as the breakthrough event which liberates us from the bondage of death. In the Letter to the Hebrews of the New Testament this point is made very clearly. Jesus is said to have entered into or seized death so that in his dying he might set free all those who from fear of death are in slavery all their lives. He has set them free from him who has had power over death, the devil (Heb. 2:14–18).

The devil, Lucifer, the ancient tempter, has had power over death and therefore the power of fear over human persons because of the successful invitation to rebel against God, to assert independence, to seize likeness to God on terms on which it was not offered. From the vantage point of Lucifer's stance, "I will not serve," death is indeed dreadful, spelling utter frustration, ridicule, annihilation or worse. When a person's existence takes this stance, then at the very least death reduces the meaning of that person's existence to absurdity. This happens not only at the moment of death, but when death is approaching. Because death is approaching all the time and we do not know when it will actually come, absurdity, fear, nausea are always ready to flood consciousness. Then life becomes an exercise in escape and delusion and the frenetic pursuit of distractions and false reassurances. Then indeed the person is enslaved to evil and is kept in that slavery by the fear of death and of all that might make one mindful of death. In this sense, human mortality and vulnerability are surely the consequence of sin.

Christian faith declares that Jesus has conquered death not only for himself but for all of us. His stance is the antithesis of Lucifer's stance. He does not grasp the likeness to God in a stance of self-assertion, but is utterly receptive to the will and call of the Father in a stance of service and obedience. His life is wholly integrated and focused toward the Father, and therefore he enters into death, the worst death, in the simplicity of answering the Father's call (Phil. 2:6–11). It is this that makes of death a consummation, a meaningful and personal act. It is this that takes away the sting of death. And it is this that takes away the fear of death that is so destructive of life and of persons. It takes away that fear for the followers of Jesus progressively as they enter more fully into the mystery and meaning of his death and resurrection. To enter into that mystery is to be wrestling with sin and sinfulness in the world.

Related Material

For a detailed explanation of the development of the notion of sin in the Scriptures, readers might turn to The Biblical Doctrine of Original Sin *by A. M. Dubarle (Herder/Seabury). For the way this was worked out in Christian Tradition and especially in the Fathers of the Church, one should turn to Piet Schoonenberg in the single volume reflecting on his more extensive research publications. The single volume in the English translation is entitled* Man and Sin, *published by the University of Notre Dame Press. The Pelagian issue, for example, is carefully explained in this volume with reference to its meaning for contemporary understanding.*

II

Jesus, the
Compassion of God

4

Jesus, Savior
and Son of God

Probably the most fundamental belief of Christians about Jesus of Nazareth is that he has come to the rescue in a hopeless situation. Christian faith begins with the experience that Jesus makes a difference. He makes the decisive difference in what we are able to hope for the world at large and for each of us in particular, both in the course of our lives and beyond death. He also makes the decisive difference in what we are able to be collectively as human community and individually as human persons.

Christian tradition gives us a rather stylized picture of who Jesus is and how and why he makes such a difference. For most of us the experience of Jesus as Savior and Son of God (Christ and Lord) is first an experience of the Church that gives testimony of him, then a quest for the elusive "real" Jesus, and finally an engagement with "the Christ of faith." This process is a little like a journey through the Gospels of the New Testament. First the Gospels present us with an interpretive account of Jesus full of allusions to the Hebrew Scriptures and to Jewish expectations. Then they confront us with the brutal fact of his death by crucifixion in a Roman execution carefully documented as to time, place, circumstance and agents. Finally they call on our faith and allegiance with the resurrection accounts.

The original Christian experience, of course, was not in that sequence. Sometimes the meaning of the Christian proclamation of Jesus as Christ and Lord really does not mean very much to people in later centuries until there is an opportunity to share in imagination the original experiences and responses out of which the official proclamations about Jesus grew. The original experience began with groups of apparently very ordinary people who became attracted in various ways and for various reasons to a wandering preacher who spoke wherever he could find people and call them together in towns, villages or the countryside. The thrust of his message seems to have been to recall them to the hope that their religious traditions in Israel gave them and to recall them to fidelity to trust and confidence in God. He spoke in ordinary language and conveyed the sense of God's presence and caring by his own human presence and caring for others and by his own human way of living his life, establishing values and priorities, praying and relating to others. He had a rousing, vivifying impact on the downtrodden poor of Roman Palestine whom he had found as listless and hopeless as the dry bones lying around on the plain in Ezekiel's vision (Ez. 37). In him—in what he was, in the way he lived and in what he said and did for them—people tended to find new life, hope, challenge, purpose in life, and healing.

For these people Jesus was so closely identified with his message that we have no record of how he looked, dressed, walked, how tall he was and so on. Of his personal habits and mannerisms, his likes and dislikes, we know only what pertains immediately to his message. From the scant evidence we have, it seems that Jesus identified himself wholeheartedly, passionately with his message, with the task that "the Father" had given him. For us Western Christians of the twentieth century there is a certain cultural gap between ourselves and Jesus of Nazareth, a first-century Jew in the land of Israel where everything had religious meaning, where the language of everyday business, farming and craft was resonant with God's revelations, where every city, village, mountain, rock and stream carried memories and promises of God's saving power, and where the daily burden of Roman domination, brutality and contempt offered a constant reminder of the great need that people had of those memories, those promises, that saving power. There is a cultural gap between our situation and that of Jesus which makes it difficult for us to catch the full impact of his preaching as his first listeners were able to catch it.

The message of Jesus had to do first of all with the powerful and compassionate fidelity of God. Living among people who were harshly oppressed, bewildered and discouraged, Jesus became for many of them the joyful discovery that God never forgets or abandons his creatures, that God is infinitely compassionate and powerful to implement his compassion in ways beyond human ingenuity and understanding. The evangelists present this message variously as the good news of the coming of God's reign or kingdom, the intimate revelation of God as self-giving Father, the uncovering of the continuing and personal providence of the Creator, and so forth. What seems to be common under these various themes is the person of Jesus himself. If Jesus preaches that "the hour of salvation" has arrived, it is because he offers himself as the turning point in human history. He offers himself, not only his words, to the people as the definitive compassion of God. He offers himself as the saving power of God which is so different from anything that we usually think of as power.

The Gospels tell us of this in the way they describe the public ministry and preaching of Jesus. They tell of his utterly generous availability to the people, particularly to their spiritual needs—their need for inspiration, hope, encouragement, guidance, challenge, correction, appreciation and attention and warm friendship—but also to their physical needs for healing and sustenance. They tell us of the circumstances, manner and content of his preaching. He preached in the open air, by the lake, on the hillsides, informally, to the ordinary poor peasant people who seem to have been despised both by the Romans and by the Jewish leadership of the time. He preached whenever people were gathered and he had the opportunity. We know that the content and manner of his preaching were very simple, appealing to the unlearned, appealing to their experience of nature and of everyday life and work. The manner and content of his preaching invited the people to become aware of God's presence and power and loving care everywhere in all things and at all times.

If the message of Jesus had to do first of all with the powerful and compassionate fidelity of God, it had to do secondly but just as essentially with the human response in which the compassionate power of God could become fruitful for the redemption of the people from the bitterness and despair of needless suffering caused by the prevailing conditions of sin. There was a transforming consolation in the preaching and presence of Jesus precisely because there was a far-reaching exigence in it. It expressed the exigence of the all-holy God on creatures whose very existence only makes sense and yields happiness and fulfillment if they direct all that they are and do and have in service, praise and gratitude to that God. This was the message of Jesus that was expressed in his person and in his life and activity. All that he said in his preaching was simply formulated in words to help others understand the simple truth of his own experience.

No doubt it was this directness and spontaneity and this self-validating quality in the preaching of Jesus that made people aware that the spirit of God was being breathed forth among them again, and that made them say of him that he taught with power. No doubt it was this also that made him a figure of contradiction. The challenge in his person called for an unconditional self-surrender. Those who would not respond to that challenge by a radical turning around of their lives, a fundamental change of consciousness and goals, could only grow to fear and hate him. Especially those whose unjust privileges and worldly pretensions were most obviously and publicly threatened could only cast about in their minds and seek counsel how to silence him effectively. Because of the way we understand power in our sinful history, the way to silence a prophet always seems to be simply to kill him. But because our sinful understanding of power is quite incorrect, this never works out as it is expected to do. The blood of martyrs is always a loud and clear witness for their cause.

Looking back after the events, the followers of Jesus began to see the difference he made, his self-definition and who and what he was in relation to God and in relation to themselves, mainly in terms of his death. They looked at the interplay of forces that brought him to his death and saw that he himself had gone to it willingly, discerning it as ultimately the only uncompromising response and self-gift to the Father and to the people, given the intractable complexity of the sinful situation and the hold that fear had over those involved. In the indescribable experience that they had of his risen presence among them and of the new life burgeoning forth in their community, everything fitted together and they began to see him at the center of history and at the heart of the mystery of God's presence in the human community. They saw him as Redeemer or Savior of the whole human situation. In his own existence Lucifer's "I will not serve" had been completely and definitively reversed in that stance of total service, the ultimate self-gift in which, paradoxically, the true image of God is dazzlingly realized and revealed (Phil. 2:6–11). But the fact that Jesus brought about this reversal of the human tragedy in his own life and person has definitively changed the human situation for the rest of us, because he has conquered the old enemy, fear (Heb. 2:10–18), and because he has made a new beginning for us (1 Cor. 15:45–49).

It is probably the train of thought just presented here that led the early Christian communities to add introductions to three of the Gospels which were not part of the original compositions. A quick comparison of the four Gospels of the New Testament (also known as the canonical Gospels to distinguish them from other gospels circulating in the early Church which did not become official) will show an important difference. The Gospel according to Mark begins with the public preaching ministry of Jesus that led eventually to his arrest, trial and execution and culminated in his resurrection and the challenge to the disciples to carry on his work. The Gospels according to Matthew and Luke have the same pattern, but each is prefaced by an introductory section consisting of the first two chapters. These are known today as the "infancy narratives." At first they seem simply to give some family details about the origins, birth and childhood of Jesus. More careful study by Scripture scholars has shown that they give rather a kind of theological statement of who Jesus is—a kind of theological statement that is quite different in style and method from the way we would do it today.

The infancy narratives tell us who Jesus is by way of story. It is a story that links him to creation and to human history, both the history of sin and the history of God's promises of redemption. The genealogies (Mt. 1:1–17 and Lk. 3:23–38) seem at first very dull reading, but when one fills in the stories behind the names one finds that the genealogies have much to say about who Jesus is. All these figures stand in the line of God's promises of redemption and are part of the process of tradition of the revelation, the hope and the response. Jesus comes as the fulfillment of it all, and this is expressed even by the symmetry of the arrangement in generations (which is artificial). A further

important part of the statement made by the genealogies
emerges from the fact that not all the persons mentioned in
them are wholly admirable people or wholly in the orthodox line
of descent. Jesus is presented as the fulfillment but not as the
predictable or merited outcome of this history. Jesus is the gift
of God that is beyond the merits of the ancestors; he is the gift
of God who is not bound by the limits and rules of the law because his very nature is to show compassion where it is neither
earned nor imagined.

An important component of what the earliest community
wanted to say about Jesus in these infancy narratives has to do
with the stylized figures of Zechariah and Elizabeth, Anna and
Simeon, Mary and Joseph. We never really find out what kinds
of people they are. They are in the story to tell us how Jesus fits
into Israel's history and expectations. Zechariah appears in the
Gospel of Luke as a priest of Israel in the course of his temple
ministry to receive the message that John the Baptist is to be the
preacher of the great authentic movement of repentance in Israel that is to prepare the Lord's way. Elizabeth is shown as el-
derly and barren, reminiscent of Sarah the wife of Abraham.
Story is laid upon story here. The child, John, is not born in the
ordinary course of Israel's history but as the special grace of
God beyond the expectations or deserts of that history, and this
child is the one who is shown later in the Gospels (Mt. 3:11–17;
Lk. 3:15–18) as the one who sums up Hebrew piety pointing to
Jesus as the coming one sent by God.

In a splendid tableau (Lk. 1:39–56) the third Gospel juxta-
poses the two highly stylized figures of Elizabeth and Mary, both
pregnant with the hope and expectation of a people in the sight
of God—the hope of Israel typified by Elizabeth bearing John,
the one who summons to repentance and points to Jesus, and
the hope of the Christian Church typified by Mary bearing Jesus,
to bring him forth as Savior in vindication of the oppressed and
lowly, the poor who trust in the power of God alone.

This is followed by the scenes presenting Joseph as the typical "just man" of Israel—Joseph whose dreams and whose Egyptian flight and exile are reminiscent of the story of Joseph the son of Jacob in the Hebrew stories of the patriarchs. The new Joseph of the Gospels is confronted with the pregnant Mary who represents the Church claiming to bring Jesus, Savior-Messiah, into the world. Joseph (just Israel) must face the problem that Mary's child, as Messiah-Savior, hope of Israel and fulfillment of the promises, is a paradox and a sign of contradiction. Israel has clearly not "fathered" him, endorsed him, authenticated his messiahship. He is a Messiah-Savior illegitimately conceived. He poses a severe problem to just Israel, to the faithful who look to God for their salvation and the fulfillment of all their hopes. In response to Joseph's anguish Mary the Church is silent because there is nothing that she can say except to bring forth Jesus into the world as Christ, showing him as he really is, the Savior "anointed" by God, coming to Israel and the world as the wonderful gift of God beyond the merits of the ancestors and preparation of the ages and the discernment of the leaders of Israel.

What the angel, the heavenly messenger or divine revelation, shows Joseph in the story is that Jesus does not need to be endorsed or authenticated ("fathered") as Messiah-Christ-Savior by Israel or its leaders. His credentials are established in heaven. The transcendent God himself has silently and mightily fathered him. His features are the living image of the invisible God. His voice is the sounding forth of the silence of God. His self-gift is recognizable as the creativity of God, and the weakness of his death becomes self-validating as the saving power of God's compassion.

Clearly, the stories themselves, as given in the Gospels of Matthew and Luke in the opening chapters, remain resolutely stories and do not launch forth into explanations such as the above. But for readers who know how to relish and meditate sto-

ries, and who are familiar with the stories of the Hebrew Scriptures, these particular simple stories and tableaux open vistas of
association, analogy, application and reflection, and through the
centuries Christian piety has indeed used and meditated the stories in this way. What is said here about the birth and the encounters that preceded the birth gives a language and a frame
of reference in which to discuss what Jesus the crucified, the ris-
en Christ, the Lord of history and coming One means to his believers and followers. When the liturgy in the cycle of the year
uses these texts, it trains our eyes to look to the future to see
God and be able to interpret our position and task in the present in relation to God. It does this on the old Hebrew principle
of meditating on the wonderful works of God in the past in symbolism and categories which make it easier for us to understand
and appropriate God's revelation to us, so that we can begin to
see the focus of God's promises in the future and discern God's
action in our present.

The Christmas story itself carries much more interpretation
and theological reflection than our modern eyes readily discern.
It is set within a situation of bitter oppression of the poor of the
world by the context that is sketched in of the taxation, the un-
seasonable compulsory journey, and the lack of accommodation
and provision for the poor and powerless people thus herded
about the country. We are told that it is from these powerless
and oppressed people that Jesus springs and that it is in these
circumstances of powerless human frustration that he emerges
in the world and into our history. The evangelists (Mt. 2:1–12;
Lk. 2:1–20) then juxtapose for us the derelict and outcast circumstances of the birth with the proclamation of it by star and
angel song. They contrast the quest for Jesus by the wise from
afar who come to do him honor with the quest for Jesus by the
power that concretely and politically holds sway over his life and
that seeks to crush and discredit him. They set the unconcern
of the world for the momentous event side by side with the hom-

age and recognition of the shepherds, the poorest of the poor in that culture, who alone were able to hear and understand the angelic announcement. They show Jesus as the great paradox of human history—the healing power of God foreordained as the center of history and its turning point, anonymous and despised if not hated. They also portray him as the Son of God in power but truly human in utter weakness.

All of this is a reflection on the identity and meaning of Jesus as it has emerged for the early community not only in his birth and childhood but also in the totality of his adult life, his death, his resurrection and his impact on his followers and on the world. All of this therefore leads naturally enough to the scenes that reflect on the relation of Jesus to the history of Israel, to its temple worship (the presentation scene) and to its wisdom and teaching (the scene of the finding in the temple). It is also summed up, so to speak, in the tableau that shows us Jesus emerging from ordinariness to assume his redemptive task in the accounts of the baptism by John in the Jordan.

In the infancy narratives of the Gospels according to Matthew and Luke, Jesus is shown to us as human in his vulnerability, his Jewish inheritance, his poverty and his humble place in society. He is also shown surrounded by an aura of divinity. Clearly, the Christian community quite early had to come to terms with what they meant when they gave Jesus titles of divinity, when they prayed to him, and when they put their whole and unconditional faith in him in a way that is really only appropriate to God. The introduction to the Gospel according to John, usually known as the Prologue, which may have been an ancient Christian hymn, reflects a further step in the question and answer about the identity of Jesus.

John 1:1–5, 9–14 and 16–18 begins by identifying Jesus with the Word of God that was with God from the beginning and through which all creatures received their being and life and light. This is an allusion to a theme of the Hebrew Scriptures.

In Genesis 1 creation is by the saying, the speech or utterance, that is, the Word of God. But this Word of God is not really a separate being but *is* God speaking. What the Prologue seems to say, then, is that the man Jesus whom the first Christians had known, seen, touched and heard came to be recognized by them as the Word or utterance of God. He is the very speaking of God in the world, the same speaking by which God has given being and life and light to creatures from the beginning. In him that Word that God is speaking has become a vulnerable, palpable human being so that God is no longer dark, silent, transcendent and terrible, but is known through Jesus as a light shining quietly in the world making God's presence known in graciousness and fidelity. Jesus is recognized as the image or reflection that gives the invisible God a face in the world. He is recognized as the Son who uniquely embodies the nature and being of the heavenly Father.

This identification of Jesus as the Word of God that was being spoken from the beginning links him with other texts of the Hebrew Scriptures, such as those which personify Wisdom and speak of it (her) as being with God from the beginning, even before the creation (for instance, Prov. 8:22–31). Such expressions in Hebrew thought suggest a polarity in God, a certain diversity and possibility of relationship, of action and of interaction even while Jews always stoutly maintained that God was absolutely and unambiguously One. When the Johannine Prologue makes this connection between Jesus and personified Wisdom, it casts an aura of mystery and of divinity over the person of Jesus. It also suggests that as the Word of God Jesus existed before his earthly, human life, and indeed beyond the boundaries of time "before the beginning of the world."

Obviously, Christians could not leave this assertion in the realm of the poetic, in the language of hints and suggestive comparisons and allusions. Very soon in the Greek thought-world of the early Church questions came pounding on the Christian consciousness and understanding about the meaning of these allusions. They were questions that were hard to answer. Some have thought both then and ever since that they were questions best left unasked because there has always been a tension between the language of faith and the language of philosophy. This tension in language reflects accurately the tension between assent to something as true because it has been revealed to us in our experience and assent to something as true because it can be logically, rationally proven.

St. Thomas Aquinas in the thirteenth century was still wrestling with that tension, as are theologians today. Aquinas was aware, and makes his readers aware, that the struggle to understand one's faith is not easily separable from philosophy but must be conducted with a proper humility. This humility consists in the first place of realizing that the truth about God and about God's dealings with us is much greater than anything we can ever hope to understand. Therefore, while there are some steps toward knowing about God which we can take on the basis of our own reasoning from observation of nature and history, they could certainly never carry us very far. But we have in fact been offered (by revelation) further knowledge of two kinds—knowledge that we might have attained by reason if our reason were not distorted by sin, and knowledge we could never have attained by reason but which offers a sure foundation for faith and understanding because it is given to us by God who shares his own wisdom and thereby offers us "first principles" or foundations on which to build a coherent and systematic human understanding.

This, of course, makes good sense to anyone in proportion to that person's faith. Without faith it sounds evasive, obscurantist and even magical in its appeal. It is largely for this reason that it is always easy to ridicule and "disprove" what Christians have believed about the meaning and identity of Jesus. There is no escaping the fact that the heart of Christian faith is in a paradox, an apparent contradiction that enshrines precious elements of Christian experience. These elements of Christian experience will not be surrendered in response to logical analysis or philosophical argument. In a sane person or a sane community deeply rooted personal experience does not yield to academic arguments that try to undermine it. But the possibility remains of exploring the truth that is received in experience in intellectual efforts to gain a deeper understanding or to integrate the apprehension of that truth in the wider sweep of one's total understanding of reality.

From early times Christians have attempted to do just this. In the earliest centuries they were very tolerant of alternate approaches used side by side. Attention focused on dealing with particular proposals that seemed to endanger Christian life and faith. St. Ignatius of Antioch in the early second century was concerned with a tendency that still affects us today—the tendency to see everything about Jesus as very ethereal and remote and not happening to a real man. In the letters he wrote on his way to Rome to be martyred, and especially in his letter to the local church at Ephesus, he addresses Christians, none of whom are old enough to have known Jesus in the flesh, and insists on the solid humanity of Jesus, a man of flesh, born of Mary, subject to suffering, and one who died. It is this flesh and blood, tangible, feeling, suffering, dying man who comes to us as a "loud scream out of the silence of God," and (in more conventional language used in the letter to the Magnesians) it is this flesh and blood man in all things pleasing to God by whom he was sent, who is the Son of the Father and the Word that goes forth from silence, in whom the Father is shown forth as a saving God.

The great Church Father, Irenaeus of Lyon, by the end of the second century was dealing with the problem of Gnosticism already mentioned in Chapter 2 of this book. This was the heresy that saw such total and irreconcilable disunity between body

and spirit, between the tangible world of our corporeal, historical and social experience and the inner world of our consciousness. Clearly, the incarnation of the divine Word in the
historical man Jesus could make no sense in a Gnostic context.
Irenaeus, of course, insists on the incarnation, that is, the realization of the divine Word in history in the flesh and blood man,
Jesus, but he goes further than that. He introduces what is
known as the "recapitulation" theme, which happens to be particularly helpful to us in our times that are so attuned to psy-
chology and the perceptions of the social sciences.

Irenaeus recalls that by sin, that is, by disobedience or turning away from God, human persons have lost their likeness to
God, and thereby the unity of the human race and indeed of the
whole creation is disrupted. The despair and sense of meaninglessness that underlie Gnosticism are precisely the reflection of
this disruption or disintegration in which matter and spirit seem
to go in contrary directions and the historical, social project of
the human race is nothing but vexation doomed to ultimate
frustration. In this context of a sinful history, Irenaeus points to
Jesus as the new head (the recapitulation) of the human community and the human project. He re-establishes God's image and
likeness and he reintegrates all dimensions of creation, physical
and spiritual, in his person in such depth and totality that he is
able to draw other persons into his own unity, undoing the destruction of original sin.

But all of this for Irenaeus is clearly by divine initiative, because the human race and the human project were too irrevo-
cably lost to be salvaged by the freedom given to the human
person in creation. The Word of God has become a man to accomplish the restoration by descending all the way into the sinful human situation even to death. In Jesus, the Word of God
becomes what we are so as to make us what he is. He does this
by being among us and instructing us. But the sublime revelation of God is realized precisely in the palpable bodily life and

death of Jesus. It is only by living according to the law and example of Jesus that one comes to experience the unity which is
the true answer to Gnosticism.

After Irenaeus, later reflection on Jesus as both human and
divine tends to focus on much more specialized and culturally
limited questions. There tended to be an interest in *how* the unity of divine and human could have come about, which is not so
helpful to Christians in their own efforts to live as followers of
Jesus. Attention began to focus not only on the question as to
how the man Jesus can be identified with the Word of God (the
Logos, in Greek) but also on the question as to how the Logos
or Word is related to the Father. One favorite answer to this latter question was that given by Tertullian, a North African who
wrote in Latin at the beginning of the third Christian century.
The Word, or eternal divine Son, is related to the Father as the
ray of sunlight is related to the sun. This image was repeated
and extended—the Son is to the Father as the shining is to the
light, as the outreach is to the source, in other words. It is an
image that still appears in the Creed of Nicea and Constantinople which is recited at the Sunday Eucharist in Catholic
churches. It is a good image. It implies unity as well as distinct-
ness. It also implies that there never was a "before" when the
Word was not.

Tertullian had apparently accepted the formulation that the
Son of God became man, so he had to explain how this could
be without his ceasing to be divine. He answered that this becoming involved a double manner of being in which the two
"substances" of the divine and the human remain intact because
they are not "poured together" or blended into one third substance but are joined so that Jesus does things that are proper
to divinity such as miracles and signs and suffers things proper
to being human like hunger and thirst and weeping and death.
But all is done by one person, one single subject. It is perhaps
unfortunate for later generations who depended rather heavily

on Tertullian's vocabulary and formula that he assigns such a purely passive role to the human, rather than a cooperative role in which human freedom and creative initiative come into play. It seems to lead Tertullian himself to see the whole mystery of the incarnation as a matter of bringing into existence a Jesus who can be made to suffer and die. Even our contemporary piety is sometimes liable to take this one-sided and rather negative view.

Clement of Alexandria, on the other hand, who wrote about the same time in Greek, is convinced that the incarnation is the expression of the overwhelming love of God who wanted to communicate himself in human form so as to gather human persons to himself in greater intimacy by teaching them that intimacy. Clement's disciple, Origen, developed these ideas in ways that were to cause difficult debates in the Church for two centuries after his death. His thought is subtle. In trying to understand what can be humanly understood of the mystery of God, Origen emphasized the spiritual, conscious, free character of the union of the Son with the Father who expresses himself in the Son or Word and that same spiritual, conscious, free character of the union of the human Jesus with the Word. Origen and his school were later accused both of making Jesus somewhat less than human, somewhat too ethereal, and of making the Word somewhat less than divine. His concern, however, was to show Jesus as a model of union with God for other human persons. In response to problems that some saw in the way this thought was developed, the fourth-century writers of the school of Antioch tried to reaffirm the fully human, historical Jesus within the teaching on the union of human and divine.

The writings of these Church Fathers of the first four centuries are full of inspiration for contemporary Christians in the following of Jesus and in prayer to Jesus, but they can also be quite confusing or misleading to contemporary Christians because they wrote in an era in which the Church had not yet agreed on a clear vocabulary or a normative set of analogies or conceptual patterns in which to speak or write about Christology. Consequently, they seem sometimes to contradict one another or even themselves and they can sometimes be badly misunderstood by the modern reader. Beginning in the year 325 at the Council of Nicea, the assembled representatives of the local churches scattered through the ancient world took up some of the questions that were troubling the faithful at that time. From a believer's point of view, this council and those which followed to the mid-fifth century were a triumph of the Spirit and the grace of God in the Church. The moving human force behind their assembling was in fact the imperial interest of Constantine and his followers, and there is plenty of evidence that they had not assimilated the teaching of the Christian Gospel in any great depth but did find the churches and their leaders a useful tool for government and administration. The teachings of these councils are not inspirational in themselves, and one could not really get an adequate picture or account of Jesus Christ from them. What they do is only to set certain ground rules or to give a frame of reference for discussion of Christology.

The Council of Nicea gave us the formulation we still have (as streamlined at Constantanople) in our Sunday Eucharist creed: we believe "in one Lord Jesus Christ, the Son of God, only begotten, born from the Father, that is, from the substance of the Father, God from God, light from light, true God from true God, begotten not made, of one nature with the Father, through whom were made all things in heaven and earth, who for us men and our salvation came down, was incarnate and made man and suffered, and rose again on the third day." The council fathers of that time were concerned about the teaching of a priest of Alexandria, Arius, and his followers who seemed to be denying the divinity of Jesus, saying there was a time when he was not, that is, before he was brought forth he was not, that he came into existence out of nothing, was different in nature from the Father, being a creature and subject to change.

Quite probably Arius was misunderstood. Much of the contemporary conflict and tension in which learned and holy theologians are being accused of heresy moves in similar patterns over familiar ground. Usually the theologian is trying to make the traditional faith and teaching meaningful and spiritually relevant to the contemporary Christian struggling to live coherently as a believer and a follower of Christ. Usually the censors who call the theologian to task are mainly concerned that the ancient formulae of words remain intact and in place. Sometimes non-theologians become quite distressed and scandalized when precisely those writers who most inspire the laity with new understanding and new motivation for discipleship and service of Jesus Christ are those constantly censored, while the theology that seems to be regarded officially as safe appears to be quite unrelated to the living of a Christian life. History is helpful. It shows that some of this tension is inevitable and even healthy. However, what is probably most helpful of all is to remember that we are in the realm of mystery where there are no formulae entirely safe from misunderstanding because there are no words and expressions that are strictly appropriate. We are always in the realm of poetic imagery.

In the decades after the Council of Nicea people seem to have felt very strongly that all their real inspiration was being ruthlessly swept away, and the following of Arius seems rather to have increased in protest than diminished in acceptance of the council. The great bishop of Alexandria, St. Athanasius, seems to have contributed significantly to the solution of this by reintroducing the very inspirational thought of Irenaeus of the second century. However, another kind of problem arose (one which also still plagues us today). A bishop by the name of Apollinaris tried to resolve the paradox of the Christian belief about Jesus by making him not quite human. It seemed to him that Jesus was simply the Word animating a human body. There is a danger of this sometimes in contemporary piety among people who think of themselves as conservative and strictly orthodox. They find it repugnant to think of Jesus as having to find things out by trial and error, having to struggle to come to a decision; the thinking and deciding seem to be divine activities, and only physical movements and physical suffering seem to be properly human. What is so bad about this is that it seems to imply that the only way that the followers of Jesus can imitate him is in passivity, not in shouldering responsibility for what goes on in the world. Apollinaris in teaching this, however, certainly did not mean to turn people away from the imitation of Jesus. He wanted to assure them that they were really saved because it was really the Word of God that had come among them and died for them. The Council of Constantinople in 381, nevertheless, ruled out this position.

The issues from previous centuries returned in the fifth century. A bishop named Nestorius had taught that the faithful should not refer to Mary as the Mother of God, but only as the mother of Jesus Christ, the man. There was a new round of efforts at a precision that was not then and will not ever be possible, but under the rubric "Mary is the Mother of God" the Council of Ephesus in 431 reasserted that we are speaking of one single subject, one single person, Jesus, the man, the divine Word. To relate to him is to enjoy a human relationship with him who is human, born of Mary, and it is also to be in immediate relationship with God present and acting in our world. Therefore, it is not inappropriate to say of Jesus Christ what may be said of the divine: we are to pay honor to Jesus Christ and place our faith in him in an unconditional way that is appropriate to the divine. Modern Christians may feel a certain im-

patience with the endless quibbling over words and the use of
words, but the issue behind them is important. It is the issue of
our way of seeking and finding salvation.

This was not the end of the matter yet. Oddly enough, the
persistent temptation for Christians through the centuries
seems to have been to resolve the essential paradox not by denying that Jesus could be divine but by denying that he was truly
human. Under the name of Eutyches and of the so-called Mo-
nophysite (one-nature) heresy, it was proposed to think and
speak of Jesus as a man who had been so absorbed into the divine that although one might speak of both the divine and the
human before, after the union the human is quite swallowed up
and ceases to have any significance. The Council of Chalcedon
in 451, to which reference is so frequently made in our times in
questions of orthodoxy in Christology, gave a resounding answer to this. Reaffirming earlier teaching of the previous councils, a letter of St. Cyril of Alexandria which had been written to
Nestorius, and a letter of Leo the Great of Rome which had been
written just two years before to Flavian of Constantinople, this
council confesses that Jesus is perfect (complete) in divinity and
perfect in humanity (that is, fully divine and fully human), truly
God and truly man with a human soul and body, one in nature
with the Father according to the divinity and one in nature with
us according to the humanity, indeed like us in all but sin, eter-
nally begotten of the Father and born in time of Mary, one
therefore in two natures (or modes of being) and not divided
into two persons nor losing the properties of the two modes of
being.

Again, much of this vocabulary, even when it has been sum-
marized, translated, and expressed in as contemporary a manner
as possible, is quite irksome to the contemporary believer. What
is truly important, however, in Chalcedon is its insistence on the
full, complete, tangible, sensitive, intelligent, responsible humanity of Jesus. This was the special agenda of Chalcedon. As

such, it was a council that foreshadowed the constant concern of New Testament scholars and theologians and preachers of our own times to make Jesus credible to believers as a man in the midst of the human community and the human situation who has indeed redeemed us and who draws us to imitate him and become one with his project in human history precisely because he is one of us and therefore can bring us into full communion with him.

Strangely, in the centuries since Chalcedon this council and its definitions have often been cited as though their primary concern had been to insist further on the divinity of Jesus. In fact, sometimes Chalcedon has been quoted and used as though it intended to insist on the divinity of Jesus at the expense of the full humanity. Sometimes, therefore, in contemporary debates about "Chalcedonian orthodoxy" it seems that the position being maintained is not so much that of the council which became normative for the Christian churches but rather that of the Monophysites against whom that council was assembled in the first place. When all is said and done, the concern of the ordinary believer, who need not be troubled by theological technicalities, is simply that in Jesus we have one who is the Savior of all, a man as human as we are but sinlessly, flawlessly focused on the heavenly Father so as to be able to gather us all into that focus, a man to whom we can turn with the trust and self-surrender that is due to God, knowing that we shall not be deceived.

Related Material

A good account of Jesus as we can know him from Scripture is offered by Bruce Vawter, This Man Jesus *(Doubleday). Vincent Zamoyta,* Theology of Christ: Sources *(Bruce), gives a selection of texts written at various times in Christian history and showing the development of thought about Christ and its formulation. For more detail on the development of Christology in the early centuries as it looks to a contemporary scholar, one might turn to Aloys Grill-meier,* Christ in Christian Tradition, *from the Apostolic Age to Chalcedon (451) (Sheed & Ward). A standard Catholic contemporary interpretation of the Catholic Christian tradition in Christology can be found in Walter Kasper,* Jesus the Christ *(Paulist Press). More provocative accounts which try to resolve some of the difficulties and unanswered questions of the contemporary believer confronted with traditional formulations of Christology are to be found, for instance, in Piet Schoonenberg,* The Christ *(Herder/Seabury), Jon Sobrino,* Christology at the Crossroads *(Orbis), which is written specifically from the point of view of socio-critical questions about salvation, and, for those prepared for extensive and heavy reading. Edward Schillebeeckx,* Jesus and Christ *(Seabury).*

5

The Death of Jesus,
Our Liberation

Perhaps the most extraordinary and puzzling claim of Christians is not that the man Jesus is truly divine, but rather that by the criminal execution of this innocent and unsuccessful man we are set free. Christians today are so accustomed to the sight of a crucifix set in a place of honor in church, school or home that they easily fail to notice how much the crucifix is really a scandal (that is, a stumbling block) to reasonable people.

All four evangelists of the New Testament are at pains to make the crucifixion the center of their teaching about Jesus. So are the letters of Paul in the New Testament and so is the Letter to the Hebrews. Early Christian piety also drew into the story of the suffering and death of Jesus some texts of the Hebrew Scriptures that had been composed long before but seemed particularly apt. These included some of the psalms and a series of texts known as the "Suffering Servant Songs" found in the Book of Isaiah (really the books of Isaiah and his school of disciples). Moreover, it is not only in the written accounts of Jesus that the death becomes central. The Eucharist, the central, constitutive action of Christian communities, has always been interpreted as bringing believers into the mystery of the death of Jesus: "This is my body which is broken for you. . . . This is my blood which is shed for you" (exact wording here taken from the *Apostolic Tradition* of Hippolytus from about the year 200), or "This is my body which is for you; do this as a memorial of me" and "This cup is the new covenant in my blood. . . . Every time you eat this bread and drink this cup, you are proclaiming his death" (1 Cor 11:24–25).

The question as to why the death of Jesus is redemptive is certainly at the core of any attempt to understand the Christian faith. The redemptive character of his death is by no means self-evident simply from the publicly accessible historical facts. If it were, there would scarcely have arisen the bitter tensions and hostilities between those Jews who rejected his messiahship and those Jews and Gentiles who accepted it and whose acceptance radically changed their whole experience and outlook on life. Nor is the answer of Christian tradition straightforward and univocal on this most important of all Christian questions. The answer arises more out of the experience of redemption than out of logical analysis. The way the answer is expressed in words is bound to reflect the historical, cultural and religious experience particular to different groups of Christians at different times and places. Because we are here so definitely in the realm in which explanations must be by analogies, images, stories and the hinting language of poetry and myth, the cultural particularity and even the individual particularity of the answers can never be resolved into one correct and universally valid answer.

This statement may surprise some, because we do have some standard Christian formulations of an answer to the question which have survived the centuries. Jesus died in obedience to the Father's will and by his obedience put right the foundationally disruptive disobedience of Adam. Jesus atoned for our sins by his innocent death. His sufferings expiated the cumulative guilt of human sin. He paid the ransom to redeem us from the enslavement of sin. The problem, however, with all of these statements is that they are perfectly clear to those who have prior knowledge and understanding of what they intend to say but are obscure and even badly misleading if offered as an initial explanation.

In order to have a clear explanation of the redemptive or liberating character of the death of Jesus, it is really necessary to proceed by way of three separate questions. First of all, who killed Jesus and why? Second, could he himself have avoided it, and if so why did he not do so? Third, how could this death possibly be seen as God's salvific will? To answer these three questions is really the task of a lifetime of reading and reflection, but also of trying to live as a follower of Jesus and praying and meditating over what one learns by doing so. Any Christian's answer to the second and third questions is necessarily very personal and rather provisional, and indeed the Church's official pronouncements on these questions over the centuries have been few and very general.

When we ask who killed Jesus and why, we find that Christians have all too often taken an extremely superficial and careless reading of the canonical Gospels, and more especially that of John, and have concluded that the "wicked Jews" killed Jesus as a blasphemer, one who insults God, while "good Christians" of course stand unequivocally on the side of Jesus, worshiping the Father "in Spirit and truth." This is a careless and irresponsible reading for several reasons. It totally ignores the story, which is told with painstaking attention to certain historical facts. It also selectively ignores the attribution of guilt that is made by the Synoptics (Matthew, Mark and Luke), and by Paul in his letters, and by John himself.

The story of Jesus in all four Gospels shows a process of polarization. Jesus announces his good news of the nearness of

the reign of God which is salvation. There is an enthusiastic response from the poor and the oppressed and a cautious response from the privileged, the rich and the powerful. The
pattern is verified again and again, and it is a pattern that we can
recognize from our own life experience. People who have found
their hope and security and future in something that is less than
and other than God receive the news of the imminence of God's
reign with quite mixed emotions. If we are quite honest in our
observations we cannot fail to notice that that includes us much
of the time and seems to have little to do with whether people
are Jews or Gentiles, Greeks or barbarians, male or female, slave
or free.

In any case, in the course of the story the polarization sharpens. Some few make a rather sweeping personal surrender to
the following of Jesus in the literal sense that they walk with him
wherever he goes on his missions of preaching and healing.
Others are drawn to him, but because they are not central in the
story we do not know the depth or the manner of their self-surrender to his good news. Others become his enemies and want
him silenced. We do not really know the membership of the various crowds that appear throughout the Gospel, but the story
seems to suggest that a large body of people is enthusiastic
about Jesus as long as his message can be interpreted in terms
of the Jewish people regaining political and military power, in
terms of the immediate (and perhaps effortless) freedom from
poverty, sickness, harsh conditions of life, and contempt. It also
seems that there is a lessening of enthusiasm whenever Jesus
makes it clear that he does not offer magical or violent solutions.

Few seem to understand what he is about when he deliberately shares the hardships and rootlessness and contempt that
are the lot of the oppressed. Even the poor and the oppressed,
who at the outset of the public ministry appear to have been so
enthusiastic, seem to abandon him as the conflict sharpens. One
may conjecture that their reason was simply that his offer of sal-

vation was not what they had at first hoped or that the terms were not as easy. The evangelists present Jesus as saying to the people in effect, "Live as I do and the kingdom of heaven will be realized among you." He gives himself, so to speak, as the pledge of the coming reign of God, but this seems increasingly improbable at the level of discernment of the things of God that his listeners are able to bring to his claim.

The actual story of the passion and death is familiar to most Christians, but it is certainly very instructive to take the Gospel accounts one by one, with a good commentary, trying to sift what the evangelist is presenting as a chronicle of events or factual record, and what he is really presenting as his or his community's theology of the events. This cannot be done here. It would be a large volume by itself, and it is in any case a volume that each Christian should, so to speak, be composing personally from personal reading, meditation and prayer. All that can be offered here is the gist of it as it appears to one Christian observer at this time.

The passion, or suffering, of Jesus seems to begin when he observes and tries to interpret the growing hostility against him and consequently sets his face to go to Jerusalem. The Letter to the Hebrews contains the extraordinary observation that he "learned obedience from the things he suffered" (Heb. 5:8). This obedience, of course, is not the execution of explicit commands; it is the discernment of the will of God for him in the complex, tangled, sinful situation in which he is called to gather up the scattered, disoriented people of God and bring them back to the true focus and meaning of their lives in the Father. Certainly both the Gospels and Christian prayers and sermons from earliest days insist that Jesus was not simply "programmed" into his death like a helpless puppet but freely came to the difficult decision to go up to Jerusalem at the volatile celebration of Passover, soberly aware that death awaited him there.

In the scenes depicting the Last Supper, the Gethsemani

vigil, and the series of trials, the evangelists give us their own reflections on what his death meant to Jesus himself. But this is within a frame of reference set up by quite factual reporting. The season is Passover time in spring when many Jewish pilgrims from the dispersion would be present. The Romans had ample guards on hand. Jesus was betrayed by one of his own, evidently a disillusioned follower. He was arrested by Jewish armed men, presumably members of the temple guard, sent by the Jewish leaders, and was brought before the high priest at night where the Sanhedrin or religious court had been assembled. The high priests and leaders involved were collaborators with the Roman occupation, holding their positions, it seems, by Roman appointment. They were people with a shrewd eye to their own interest and safety, and not necessarily at all devout. According to Mark, it was their anxious concern to find out whether Jesus claimed to be the Christ, in the Hebrew form as transliterated, the Messiah (that is, the anointed or chosen by God). This would imply that he had a mission to bring salvation to the people, and that was at the time commonly interpreted as including liberation from Roman rule, probably by military uprising. Matthew and Luke agree with this account of what it was that constituted the interest of the Jewish leaders. All three evangelists then assert that Jesus was led off a prisoner and turned over to the Roman governor, Pontius Pilate. Luke fills in the detail of the charge, saying that Jesus was denounced as a rabble-rouser who forbade payment of taxes to the Roman conquerors and who claimed to be Messiah.

Though the role of Messiah was in the first place a religious idea, it was bound to be of interest to the Roman conquerors because it was quite commonly expected that Messiah would be a military leader, and indeed there were from time to time claimants to the role who tried to organize a rebellion. Actually, it appears that Jesus himself did not claim the role of Messiah during his lifetime, though his disciples later gave him that title, so that we know him as Christ (which means Messiah) almost as though that had been his surname, and it seems to us that he must always have been so named. If Jesus himself did not claim the title of Messiah, that seems to be for several reasons. First of all, because of the popular military connotations it could be quite misleading to his followers. Second, he was not concerned with claiming any titles, because his focus was not on himself but on the coming reign of God among human persons. Third, the mission and the person of Jesus in history were unique and there was no pre-existing category into which he could be slotted. Besides this, it is quite clear that when his followers gave him this title after his death and resurrection, they changed the meaning of the title by making it more explicit and also more universal in application than it was in Jewish usage.

If we were to follow the reported conversations between Pilate and the Jewish leaders and Pilate and Jesus, as well as the story of the trek across Jerusalem to Herod, we would be impressed with the evangelists' insistence that neither Pilate nor Herod could find matter on which to condemn Jesus. But it is difficult here to be sure of what is unadorned chronicle and what is Christian meditation on the injustices and ironies of the process, cast in dialogue form. What is undeniable fact is that Jesus was condemned and executed by order of the Roman governor, in the particularly torturing, horrifying way that was considered appropriate to those who constituted a threat to Roman rule and order. The reason for the execution, tacked over his head on the wooden cross, read: "This is the king of the Jews." That Jesus was killed by the Romans because they feared that sooner or later he would undermine their (unjust) power is further confirmed by the story of Barabbas and by the story of the mocking soldiers and the crown of thorns. In the Barabbas story Pilate offers to observe the Passover custom of releasing one popular (political) prisoner. In the crown of thorns story a charade is described that had been inflicted on other Jewish prisoners by Roman soldiers, apparently working off some of their fear and frustration in a highly flammable situation in which everything in Jewish tradition and consciousness challenged the injustice of the Roman occupation.

Taking all the evidence together, there can be no doubt that the Romans killed Jesus because they saw him as a threat to their oppressive rule. In all of the above, the passion story in the Gospel according to John has not been used. In its presentation, that story seems to place much more of the responsibility for the death on the Jews, showing Pilate almost as a helpless puppet. John's Gospel, however, has to be read as commentary on the other three (much earlier) Gospels. It is much less concerned than the other three to tell the story of Jesus as it happened and much more concerned than they to reflect on it theologically. It is much more concerned to answer the second and third questions with which this chapter is concerned than the first. Moreover, John's Gospel is written in the light of what has happened to the young Church in two or three generations after the death and resurrection of Jesus. It is also written in a context in which the Christian communities are still very largely composed of Jews who have acknowledged Jesus as the Messiah sent by God. In such a context, what is said about Jews should be read as saying: our own people did this; precisely the official representatives of the true faith were guilty of this treachery; standard piety is proved wanting by the execution of Jesus. In other words, if we move from the question of fact, concerning who killed Jesus, to the value judgment of the attribution of guilt, the answer of the evangelists and of Paul in his letters is a very comprehensive one and is not in the third person. Not "they" but "we" bear the collective responsibility, because the stories show that all the respectable, law-abiding, prudent and even pious options that the various parties to the drama can take stand condemned before the cross of Jesus. They stand condemned as evasive, self-serving, ungenerous and not ultimately obedient to God.

Because the historical evidence is clearly that of a Roman execution of one thought to be a threat to Roman rule, the question arises urgently (and has been much discussed in the twentieth century) whether Jesus did in fact preach or intend a military uprising, and, if he did not, how the shrewd Roman governor whose position and life depended on his making sound judgments could have been so badly mistaken. On the first half of this question the evangelists leave us no doubt at all. They insist that he would not let himself be taken and made king by popular acclaim. They insist that when asked about taxes to Caesar, he made an important distinction and did not forbid payment of taxes. Time and again they show him reproving his followers for playing with ideas of violence. Most decisively, they show him as making no resistance to his arrest and not allowing his followers to make any resistance either. When the title of Messiah is claimed for Jesus posthumously, it has been stripped of military connotations.

The other half of the question, how the Roman governor could have been so mistaken, is more subtle. Even if Jesus was committed, as he does indeed seem to have been, to total non-violence, that does not necessarily mean that he is to be seen in the broad sense as non-political. The preaching and personal stance of Jesus certainly invited people to live beyond fear, beyond selfish disregard for others, beyond greed and lust for personal power. Every unjust and oppressive regime is heavily dependent on the fear of the oppressed which prevents them from acting as a community or on behalf of one another simply because no one wants to take any risk for the benefit of others. Unjust and oppressive rule is almost always dependent on the greed, selfishness and lust for power of some collaborators from among the oppressed group, middlemen who gain some small, miserably disproportionate personal advantage by betraying and oppressing their fellows. Oppression is also usually dependent on a sense of utter powerlessness in which people persuade

themselves that they have no moral obligations because they
have no freedom of choice or any power in the shaping of the
society.

It would seem that the preaching of Jesus to the poor and
the oppressed of Israel directly confronted these attitudes with
a call for radical conversion from fear, selfishness and greed,
which was a call toward genuine and responsible community.
This suggests that we should not too readily assume that his
non-violent stance was a totally non-political stance. The political sphere can be seen in narrow or broad terms. Party politics
such as we know them did not, of course, exist at that time. Jesus
did not live in a democracy, nor in a situation in which the rulers
held themselves accountable to the people in any constitutional
or political sense. But even the harshest military dictatorship
rests to some extent on the willing or unwilling consent of the
governed. To live beyond fear or to live ultimately accountable
to a higher authority is to put limits on the power of a dictatorship, and to bring about modifications of the political structures.

The question which the earnest follower of Jesus is much
more interested in asking, and which some readers will have
waited for with increasing impatience, is the second question of
this chapter, namely whether Jesus could have avoided this particularly awful death so early in his public ministry, and, if he
could, then why he walked on to Jerusalem and right into the
trap. The first half of this question, as mentioned earlier, both
the Gospels and Christian piety (as expressed in liturgical texts
and sermons from early days) answer unhesitatingly. The Gospels offer numerous texts in which Jesus explicitly says that he
is going up to Jerusalem where he will be condemned to death
(Mt. 16:21; 17:22–23; 20:17–19; Mk. 10:32–34; Lk. 18:31–34).
When Peter tries to persuade him otherwise, Jesus tells him:
"You think as men think, not as God thinks" (Mt. 16:22–23).
The refrain of the Holy Week liturgy, as of Christian meditation

on the passion of Jesus, has been: "Quia ipse voluit"—he suffered by his own free will; he assented to this.

The other half of the question, namely, why he assented to it, is more subtle. The Gospels give us only indirect help in this. There is, of course, the Gethsemani scene with the utterance of the agonizing prayer to the Father, "Not my will but thine be done." But that tells us only the conclusion of the process of discernment by which Jesus came to the decision to allow himself to be arrested, condemned and brutally tortured to death. If we want to attempt some understanding of that process of discernment itself, perhaps the most important insight comes from the story of the temptations faced by Jesus in the desert.

The story of the temptations in the desert is a very stylized and allusive presentation of the outlook of Jesus on his own mission. The story is told in Matthew 4, Mark 1 and Luke 4, the Marcan account being very brief and the other two almost identical except for the order in which the temptations are given. The three "temptations" in the story are certainly classic issues for the people of Israel and classic questions about their expectation of Messiah, God's anointed sent to save them. The setting is the desert, traditionally the trysting place of human persons both with God and with the devil, the place of naked confrontations and drastic decisions. The desert is also reminiscent of Israel's beginnings as a people, its time of instruction and training by its God, and in a sense it recalls the halcyon days of Israel's honeymoon period of fervor and simplicity. Saints and prophets had then, and have since then, been shaped by the desert experience. The temptation story tells us that Jesus was in the desert fasting for forty days and nights. Israel, of course, was said to have wandered in the desert forty years, utterly dependent on God for its sustenance. But more immediately the reference is to both Moses and Elijah, each of whom fasted in solitude for forty days. The biblical sense of a fast is that it is an expression of humility before God, an attitude of dependence, an act of total abandonment to God. Devout Jews fasted before undertaking an important or particularly difficult mission or task. It was their way of putting the matter wholly in God's hands.

With this background, the forty-day fast in the desert by Jesus at the outset of the public ministry comes into focus as the expression of his radical dependence on, and abandonment to, the Father. In that context there is a battle of spirits, of Satan, the tempter or evil spirit, challenging the Holy Spirit by whom Jesus has been led into the desert, the trysting place. The root meaning of temptation is "trial" or "test." The first temptation as given by Matthew is to relieve the ordinary human need of hunger (or, more correctly, starvation) by miraculous power, but the answer of Jesus (just completing the long fast which is his gesture of total abandonment to the Father) puts the question in a larger context. The meaning of his mission goes further than caring for physical needs, even when these are desperate as at the point of starvation, because the real and deepest need, hunger, even starvation, of the human race is not merely for bread but for the creating, revealing, transforming Word of God. This answer, of course, would horrify us with its callousness if it did not come from a man who had just observed a total fast for forty days, a man who then set out to share the deprivations, sufferings, indignities, insecurity and powerlessness of the oppressed even to their bitterest end in a terrible torture death. The same answer rolling glibly from the tongues of well-fed, well-clad, comfortably housed, and carefully protected preachers and academics would seem to be precisely un-Christian, the very antithesis of all that Jesus means for salvation.

The second temptation described by Matthew is an invitation to ensure a following by spectacular and overwhelming signs, attempting to force the hand of God to obey human designs in rampant disregard of the responsibility that is the other side of human freedom. The answer of Jesus seems to say that it is for God to command and test human beings, not for human beings to command and test God. The last temptation in Matthew's recital is to a messiahship according to worldly power. Even more than the other two, this temptation is worded so symbolically that it leaves us great latitude to project our own interpretations. Some have even interpreted it to mean that the true mission of Jesus and his followers is in the broadest sense non-political (that is, unconcerned with structures of society that oppress people, and unconcerned with poverty as a social phenomenon, with war, with racial oppression and in general with social responsibility). The subsequent ministry of Jesus and its consummation in his arrest, Roman condemnation and Roman execution, as well as the subsequent history of the early Church, should suggest the greatest caution concerning any such "privatized" interpretation.

There is much to suggest that these "temptations" of Jesus in the desert are not so much concerned with his expectations concerning his ministry as with his followers' expectations even down to our times and down to us. Salvation by bread, by evolution, by technical progress, by increasing production, without any need of renunciation for others on the part of the over-privileged, is hope to which those of us who call ourselves Christian today constantly find ourselves clinging or returning. Salvation by magic tricks, without any real need of total conversion, whether it be salvation by ritual, or by a formula of words proclaiming faith in Jesus as Savior, or by inducing ecstatic feelings of being saved, has been a constant temptation among Christians just as it was among Jews. The temptation to seek salvation by worldly manipulations of people by external sanctions and the wielding of governmental structures of power was by no means confined to Constantine and his followers in the fourth century but is a constant temptation of all who hold authority in the Church as of all who look to authority as mediating God's saving power to them.

If, however, these temptations are more a stylized scene depicting the stance that Jesus took than a simple chronicle of specific problems he wrestled with, they nevertheless underscore the inexorable logic by which Jesus moved through the actual steps of his public ministry to his death as the outcast of society, the one who did not count, who could safely be disregarded, who could be made the butt of everyone's frustration and pent-up anger. The answer that the evangelists Matthew and Luke put in the mouth of Jesus after the third temptation seems to link the whole scene and the whole ministry of Jesus with the stories of the "sin of the angels" and the sin of Adam. The task of discernment is to read rightly what is worship of God and what is idolatry, the acknowledgement of absolute claims on the part of anything and anybody that is not God. In fact the answers to all three temptations are, in a sense, the same as the answer to Peter that was mentioned above: this is the logic of the way (sinful) men think, not the logic of God.

The task of salvation that Jesus undertakes is to reverse the "non serviam" of Lucifer, the disobedience of Adam, and all the structures of bullying and self-seeking and greed that flow from these. The whole career of Jesus as well as his death seems to say that one cannot defeat these enemies by joining them in the use of their own strategies of power. The only power that can hold the victory over them is the power of God that is exercised in utter humility, trust, dependence and self-abandonment to the Father. The way Jesus carries this out is not, however, in effortless passivity nor by uncritically fulfilling the role in which society had cast him. Clearly he was not crucified for conducting himself as a good Jewish carpenter in Nazareth. Shrewd people who had everything at stake in making a correct judgment in the

matter estimated that his way of conducting himself was danger-
ously, pervasively, politically subversive.

When we inquire further what was his way of conducting
himself that brought him so inexorably to that terrible and ig-
nominious death, we find that it was in the first place the way
of the prophet. The prophet speaks in season and out of season,
until his words ring in people's ears and consciences, the judgment of God on the human situation in all its tragedy and sinfulness. But the prophet does not threaten; he warns. The
judgment of God is not in the imposition of extrinsic sanctions
or arbitrary punishments, but in the revelation of the intrinsic
consequences of sin and of the every-ready outreach of God to
turn human hearts back to him if they will let him. Jesus said this
so convincingly because he said it with his whole life and being,
because he said it non-violently without bullying or threat but
also without toning down in the least the urgency and ultimacy
of the warning, and because he said it out of personal experience from the midst of the human situation, even from the utmost depths of human misery and helplessness that can be
inflicted on a human being. He went to the poor, the oppressed,
the most despised, and he went all the way.

When Christian piety has reflected on this story in its many
facets, it has answered the question as to why he did it in a very
simple statement; he did it out of pure love, love in the first
place of the Father, which in the second place is quite inseparable from love for fellow human beings. This love of the Father
consists in perfect obedience in the sense that it discerns without distortion or evasion what it is that will implement the salvific will of God, that is, the compassionate power of God, in the
world in all its sinful complexity. The man, Jesus, becomes
wholly the compassion of God.

The foregoing already suggests the main lines according to
which Christian thought through the ages has attempted to an-

swer the further crucial question of this chapter, namely, how this death of Jesus can possibly be seen as the salvific will of God. The first step of the answer to this is certainly in the refrain of Christian worship, "Quia ipse voluit," because the decision was taken by Jesus in the utmost personal freedom in his response of filial self-abandonment into the hands of the Father and in his dedication of himself to others to be the compassion of God for them. The second step of the answer is that he recapitulates or incorporates in himself the whole human community, making it possible for all of us to turn back to God because he has done it in such a radical, such a foundational way. This is the recapitulation theme of St. Irenaeus of the second century which was mentioned in the previous chapter, though it had its origin in the thought of St. Paul (Eph. 1:10).

Out of the idea that Jesus became what we are to make it possible for us to become what he is, and the idea that Jesus plays the role of a second Adam by reversing the damage done, incorporating us into himself, turning sin and death into true life and immortality, restoring God's image and likeness in the human community, comes also the language of ransom. Jesus conquered the power of the devil by paying our ransom from the devil with his blood. All these images clearly point to the sense in which the self-sacrificing death of Jesus can be said to be the will of God. Tertullian in the third century introduced the idea that sin imposes an obligation of satisfaction made to God. Combining these and some other strands of patristic thought, the theology and piety of the West worked itself into some false dilemmas to which we today fall heir. Taking the notion of satisfaction and the notion of ransom perhaps too seriously, or too literally, some Christians wasted much speculation on whether the ransom for our liberation from sin was paid to the devil or to God.

That involved the following dilemma. If the ransom was paid to the devil, then it would seem that by evildoing a creature could acquire rights against God. This is patently absurd and would take us into Gnosticism or Manichaeism in which there is an independently creative and independently powerful principle from which evil and darkness flow. It is for this reason that Anselm of Canterbury in the eleventh century responded most emphatically that the ransom could not possibly have been due to the devil, but must have been paid to God whose holiness and majesty were offended (insulted) by sin. That, however, becomes the other horn of the dilemma, inasmuch as it tends to suggest a defensiveness, even a petty vengefulness on the part of God, that is not at all like the Father of Jesus, the God whose power is his compassion. Subsequent theology tried to deal with this by another analogy from the structures of human society as then experienced: an offense is said to be measured by the dignity of the one offended, reparation of the offense by the dignity of the one who offers it. Therefore, Jesus being both divine and human is able to offer infinite reparation for the offense against the infinite dignity of God, and thus the willing death of Jesus is at the same time the full satisfaction of the human race offered by its proper representative and the compassion of God who comes to the rescue.

This explanation could never satisfy contemporary believers, because it does not even reflect our perception of human society and seems altogether too contrived and legalistic to express the truth of Jesus as our salvation. The same must be said even more emphatically of the predominantly Protestant notion of the substitutionary death of Christ. Yet it would seem that the intent of Anselm and those who followed him can be expressed in language that the contemporary Christian can recognize as dealing with the reality of our lives in the world as we know it.

Just as we understand original sin to be more than a legalistic attribution of guilt, but rather as a distortion and diminishment that affects all aspects of our existence, so the meaning of redemption in Jesus Christ is more than a legalistic attribution of justice or righteousness. There is indeed a ransom to pay for sin in the sense that turning from habits of selfishness, domination, timid compromises and so forth carries an intrinsic cost of human suffering simply in renunciation, asceticism and acting contrary to inclination, comfort and convenience. This is so even in the act of turning individually from a personal stance or habit of sin. It is compounded in the social context of a history of sin, where the structures and values and expectations of society and therefore its rewards and punishments are largely set in opposition to God. We can see that in our times in the patterns that draw people as helpless victims into alcoholism and drug abuse. We can see it in the discouragingly intractable patterns of racial discrimination that survive generation after generation and martyrdom upon martyrdom and still seem untouched. We can see it also in the appalling extent of starvation and abject destitution in a world where adequate resources are kept from distribution by interlocking systems of mass self-interest. Similarly, we see it in situations in which inadequacies or distortions in the character of parents, for which they themselves are not to blame, nevertheless damage their children psychologically and socially for life so that they in turn damage others.

These are situations in which the individual is helpless because there is no way in which an individual can pay the cost, offer the ransom, that will turn the situation. They are often situations in which society as a whole is helpless, because everyone in society is compromised by self-interest, security, identity, and recognition from others, which depend precisely on the sinful structures as sinful. The laws and government of society are at best an uneasy compromise holding injustices, selfishness, cruelty and violence within some sort of predictable bounds. Those of us who are privileged (over-privileged) in our societies are apt to be slow to recognize this, but those who are the oppressed, the excluded, the marginated and the powerless are bitterly and keenly aware of it as the pervasive condition of social life.

What Christians claim is that Jesus has in principle effectively turned this situation around, making a new beginning, restoring the image of God, paying the price or ransom in this metaphorical sense, in such a way that he is able to incorporate all human beings into his own stance of openness to God and to others. Jesus has been able to do this first of all in his own person because he is sinless and therefore not held bound by the uneasy compromises on which inauthentic identity and security always rest. He has been able to do it because in utter freedom and unconditionally he gave himself in his full humanity to the Father to be the expression in the world of his creative and redemptive Word. But he has been able to do it also because as the divine Word he gave himself in sublime simplicity and uncalculating generosity to his fellow human beings as sustenance for the true identity, the true purpose in life, the true security which they had lost.

The death of Jesus is more than a good example of unselfishness to inspire us. It is more than a demonstration of the self-giving compassion of God made visible upon the stage of human history to encourage us to turn to God in repentance. The death of Jesus is a reorientation of human freedom to God so fundamental and consequential that it constitutes a kind of cosmic explosion of possibilities which definitively alters the whole human situation.

Related Material

The sources in Christian tradition for working out a contemporary understanding of the Christian doctrine of redemption have been gathered in a very helpful selection by John R. Sheets, The-ology of the Atonement: Readings in Soteriology *(Prentice-*

Hall). The link between soteriology (that is, redemption theology) and Christology (more usually concerned with questions of the identity of Jesus in relation to the Father and in relation to the human community and the world) becomes very clear in another selection from the Fathers of the Church by James M. Carmody and Thomas E. Clarke, Word and Redeemer *(Paulist Press). A similar collection with a similar purpose was made by Piet Smulders,* The Fathers on Christology *(St. Norbert Abbey Press).*

Many contemporary books on Christology have approached the topic from the point of view of the work of Jesus as Savior. Perhaps the most important is that of Schillebeeckx already mentioned. A number of third world writers, especially from Latin America, known as liberation theologians, have attempted to give the Catholic understanding of Jesus as Redeemer in terms of the contemporary felt needs of redemption and the contemporary realization of the social and institutional pattern of sin in the world. Typical and available in English are Jon Sobrino, Christology at the Crossroads *(Orbis), Leonardo Boff,* Jesus Christ the Liberator *(also Orbis), and John Desrochers,* Christ the Liberator *(Centre for Social Action, Bangalore, India) which contributes an Asian perspective to the discussion.*

6

The Resurrection,
Foundation for Our Hope

All of the foregoing chapter has been carefully written without reference to the resurrection, not because the resurrection is unimportant (for it is the central doctrine of Christian faith) but because it is so easy to misunderstand the resurrection at a very superficial level that bypasses the question of what is at stake in the redemption from sin and death.

The doctrine of the resurrection of Jesus, as anticipation of a general resurrection, has been so clearly central since the earliest days of Christianity that Paul was able to write without any qualification that if there had been any mistake on this point, if Christ had not been raised, his preaching and his readers' faith would be in vain, for they would still be in their sins (1 Cor. 15:14–18). Because the whole faith revolves around this assertion of the resurrection of Jesus, it is important to understand that assertion in the fullness of its biblical allusions and in the wide range of its resonances and implications.

In the passage just cited, Paul makes the point that the resurrection of Jesus is inextricably bound up with the universal destiny of the human race, with the hope and purpose in life of each and all of us. In his death, willingly accepted in pursuit of his mission, Jesus defined himself as pure love of the Father and of his fellow human beings. Yet his mission of the ushering in of the reign of God, of final peace and salvation and fulfillment for human persons, is so intimately connected with his personal life and being that the disciples were not altogether wrong when they responded to his death with dumb despair. They saw more clearly perhaps than anyone before or since then that the meaning and purpose of human lives is not disclosed in the sequence of events in history that lead up to death. The lives of martyrs for any cause, of the good and generous who sacrifice themselves for others, beg the question of a vindication by God if human life and experience is not ultimately absurd.

In this context, the resurrection of Jesus is the great central revelation of Christian experience and history. It is the burning bush of Christians. Just as the story of the burning bush in the life of Moses and the people of Israel is much more than a testimony of an isolated event inexplicable by natural causes and taken to guarantee a religious message, so the resurrection of Jesus is much more than the testimony of such an isolated event breaking the laws of nature to guarantee the message of Jesus. The burning bush of Moses is precisely the paradigm or type in which the people are to recognize how God reveals himself in the new life that bursts forth out of suffering fidelity. The burning bush is not a proof of anything, but it is a sign of God's compassionate power at work in human history and destiny, drawing it to a wonderful fulfillment. So the resurrection of Jesus is not a proof of anything, but it is a sign of the compassionate power of the Father vindicating and fulfilling the human self-oblation of Jesus in a transforming radiance of divine splendor and peace which guarantees the meaning and purpose not only of the life and death of Jesus but of all human life and death. It is an "es-

chatological" sign. That is to say, it points to a goal and fulfillment lying beyond historical scrutiny.

Like the burning bush, the resurrection of Jesus does not
offer proof of anything because it is not a publicly evident event
testified by neutral observers. It is a believers' testimony to believers. The New Testament is rather insistent about this. Its
general tenor is that the proof of the truth or reliability of the
resurrection claim is the profound and otherwise inexplicable
change that has come about in the Christian communities.
Sometimes Christians of later ages have missed this emphasis
because of a too superficial reading of the proclamations of the
resurrection and the stories about the resurrection. A careful
reading will show immediately that there are many contradictions in these texts. This is important as a clue to the way the
original writers and compilers intended their texts to be understood. If they had intended to present to their readers accounts
that were to be taken as a literal chronicle of events as they were
observed, then these writers and compilers would surely have
sifted their sources carefully to determine which version was
more accurate or more likely to be accurate. Yet they make not
the slightest attempt at this and appear to have been untroubled
by all the contradictions. They seem simply to have aimed at a
collection of the available resurrection faith proclamations and
resurrection appearance stories without concern about inconsis-
tencies. That tells us that they thought faith would be nourished
by looking at the resurrection from all these different points of
view, and that they had something in mind that went beyond the
chronicling of events.

Actually, as far as specialists are able to trace the oral
preaching which came before the written testimonies and on
which those written testimonies were based, it would seem that
the earliest proclamation used several models or images in
speaking about what had happened to Jesus after his death and
burial, one of which was the image of exaltation or being lifted

to divine heights, to heavenly glory (as in Phil. 2:6–11 and 1 Tim. 3:16), and another of which was that of being raised from the sleep of death and released from the tomb (as in Peter's Pentecost sermon in Acts 2:23–24). Both images allude to texts and stories of the Hebrew Scriptures and to the non-biblical traditions and teachings of Israel. The plurality and allusive character of this imagery tells us something more that is important. When biblical authors have no exact language to describe or tell something, they frequently use a number of different analogies, images, symbols. Sometimes they even use them paradoxically, that is, in apparent contradiction to each other. It is a way of letting the listener or reader know that the texts are not intended to be taken literally but are meant to be suggestive, to hint at something that cannot be said in strictly appropriate terms. This by no means indicates that the reality is less than is being said. It always indicates that the reality is more than is being said.

Resurrection of the dead in the messianic era was already a way of expressing Israel's hope and trust in God in the intertestamentary period before Jesus. That is why the Gospels report an argument of Jesus with the Sadducees over the issue of resurrection (Mt. 22:23–33) and the Acts of the Apostles show Paul taking sides with the Pharisees against the Sadducees on the same issue (Acts 23:6–8). The general sense of this expectation was that it answered the bewilderment of those Jews who saw in distress that precisely the most faithful servants of God seemed to die abandoned, tormented, disinherited, discredited and tortured to death by successive conquerors of Israel. In response to this the scribes or rabbis could only insist that God is not less faithful than human persons. Therefore it must be supposed that when his day comes, the day of his victory in which he vindicates the poor who put their trust in him, he will surely rouse the faithful from their tombs and lead them into the rejoicing throng to participate in the victory.

This way of speaking gives content to hope by drawing the

analogy between sleep and death, between getting up in the morning and a newness of life that is beyond death. The image does not really claim to tell anything of what this "beyond death" is like. It simply reasserts utter confidence in the fidelity of God. The basis in experience for that confidence is the fidelity of God in creation as known in the cycle of sleeping and waking and the fidelity of God in grace, in his Spirit, as known in one's own human fidelity. It is not conceivable that God could be less faithful than human persons. Jesus, in the passage cited above, heartily endorses this rabbinic teaching as giving a trustworthy expression to the hope of salvation and vindication by God the Father.

The New Testament texts of exaltation and resurrection do not claim to tell us what Jesus himself experienced beyond his death. They only claim to tell us how his followers experienced the judgment or vindication of the Father in relation to Jesus beyond the scandal and despair of his death, and how this vindication became for them a new definition of who Jesus was and a new definition of who they were. They testify that they were left in a state of helpless stupor by his execution and had no sense of purpose or direction or divine providence at that time. Then in a variety of ways they tell us that something happened that was in the strictest sense ineffable, that is, something that simply cannot properly be put into words. But they try to tell us what it is that happened indirectly in three ways. The first way is the living response and transformation of the scattered and disillusioned followers of Jesus who become the community of his presence and his saving power in the world. The second way is by proclamation of what Jesus has become for them, of the way they now understand his identity, his relation to the Father and his relation to them and to the whole human race. The third way is by a series of stories of his impact on his believers, stories of appearances, of his teaching and enlightening them, of his commissioning them with an apostolic task in the world, of his promising to be with them and to meet them at the end of their task, and stories of journeys to and from an empty tomb.

All these stories and proclamations are gathered together in the ways in which various preachers, writers and compilers thought they would best explain the good news of salvation in Jesus as the Christ. We do not have them in the New Testament in the order of their composition. What is earlier in the collection of documents in the New Testament may be much later in its original composition as a way of expressing the Easter faith of the community. The cumulative effect is to tell us that they know from their own experience that Jesus lives and that his life and mode of existence are not simply a matter of resuscitation in order to continue to live the same life, but a radical breakthrough to a new dimension of life. His new and transformed life has become so pervasive, so liberating and sustaining, so internal to their own freedom and their own consciousness, that Paul is able to say of himself and of all believers that the energy and power of Christ is at work in them (Col. 1:29), that they have become members of Christ's body (Col. 1:28) and that they have died and been raised to new life in him (Col. 3:1–4). Moreover, this experience that he lives in a new dimension has been such that they now see him as the "image of the invisible God," the principle by which and for which all things are created and all creation is held together in harmony (Col. 1:15–20). It is this experience that leads them to address Jesus with the divine title of Lord and speak of his sitting at the right hand of the Father (Acts 2:34–36).

This has always been for Christians the central image of hope, the pledge of a fulfillment yet to come, the "first fruits" of the redemption. Ignatius of Antioch, writing early in the second century on his own way to martyrdom, writes of the testimonies of the resurrection as the strength of martyrs on account of which they despised death. Polycarp, a little later, writes in a similar vein of the resurrection of Jesus as grounding the hope of the faithful for their own resurrection and grounding also the joy of their present life even in persecution. Irenaeus see Jesus, the risen One, as the principle and guarantee of the restoration and re-creation of all things because he became what we are to make us what he is, and the resurrection is the crossing by which he leads us out from slavery. Origen in the third century sees our resurrection in and with Christ as something that happens in stages, being already partly accomplished but pointing forward to future completion.

St. Athanasius and St. John Chrysostom, both in the fourth century in the Eastern Church, emphasized the Christian understanding of the resurrection of Christ as the victory over sin and death, for it takes away the terror of death that entraps human beings and holds them enslaved (as mentioned earlier in reference to the Letter to the Hebrews of the New Testament). St. Augustine in the fifth century in the Western Church sees the resurrection as the definitive conquest of the power of the devil that brings about (causes) our redemption. In general, for the Church Fathers, the resurrection of Jesus is not only the first fruits of a harvest yet to be gathered in, but is already the resurrection of the human race in a seminal way. We are all already affected by it. But the risen Christ and his impact are known by faith, not by study or research into historical testimony. His presence is a matter of personal experience in the transformed life and relationships of the community of believers which is the Church. That community mediates the presence of the risen Jesus and therefore is the body of the risen Christ in the world.

Subsequent theology until recent times has perhaps not given enough attention to the resurrection and its meaning in the redemption of the world, though Thomas Aquinas in the thirteenth century saw it as the cause of our redemption and as the immediate cause of the Church and its sacraments. Unfortunately, apologetics (the disciplined argumentation in defense of the faith) in modern times tended to answer materialistic and reductionist objections to the truth claim of the resurrection with materialistic and reductionist defenses of that truth claim which cheapened the sense of mystery (that is, inexhaustible truth) and of theophany (that is, the revelation of the divine) in the resurrection. More recently, popularizations of exegetical (that is, detailed textual) studies of the New Testament have focused popular attention on the one question whether the tomb was really found empty or whether that was a manner of expressing the experience that Jesus had been delivered from death by the Father into a new dimension of life. This also seems to trivialize the mystery of the resurrection by turning attention away from its spiritual significance, that is, its import for Christian life in faith, hope and charity, and turning attention instead toward the satisfying of idle curiosity. It seems to shrink the resurrection from dimensions of universal revelatory and saving force sending explosive energy through all creation, reducing it to an isolated remarkable incident that eludes explanation according to our knowledge of the laws of nature.

The resurrection of Jesus seems to tell us that the power of God working within human freedom transcends death. It is a healing and not a vengeful vindication of the poor and oppressed and lost and bewildered. It demands a radical conversion of our human understanding of power and victory. It liberates at levels of human experience and in dimensions of human existence where we did not even have sense enough to suspect how enslaved we were. The resurrection of Jesus is something we have not really begun to understand yet because it anticipates the end and goal of all our human history and beckons us toward our final consummation in God. The way toward understanding it is certainly by participation in the cross of Jesus which is the bridge across death to the risen life of the new creation. That is why the Eucharist is at the heart of the Church.

Related Material

A rather careful summary of the biblical and traditional testimonies and teachings about the resurrection of Jesus is given in Walter Kasper, Jesus the Christ *(Paulist Press), and a discussion of the New Testament texts in detail is available in Raymond Brown,* The Virgin Birth and Bodily Resurrection of Jesus *(also Paulist Press). A helpful selection of the writings of the Church Fathers on the topic is available in Thomas P. Collins,* The Risen Christ in the Fathers of the Church *(Paulist Press).*

A very extensive meditation on the implications of the biblical texts on the resurrection is offered by F. X. Durwell, The Resurrection *(Sheed & Ward). A brief but incisive reflection on the resurrection of Jesus and that of Christians is to be found in the sections on those topics in Josef Ratzinger,* Introduction to Christianity *(Herder/Seabury).*

III

The Spirit
in the Church

7

The Church as
Communion and Institution

What most puzzles many outsiders and most embarrasses many insiders about the Catholic faith today is the account that the Church gives of itself. Symbolic or representative of the two poles or foci of this discomfort are the roles played by Mary the Mother of Jesus and by the Pope, successor of Peter and bishop of Rome. The two figures express the living paradox of the Church's identity, its inspiration and its life. They express a tension which is not an accident of history that has happened to arise in our present cultural situation but that is the necessary condition of being the Church in the unredeemed world.

All that the Church claims and teaches about its own mission and character is in answer to the question raised for the first disciples by the death, resurrection and ascension of Jesus. The story of Jesus might have been complete with the testimony of the resurrection and the general theme of exaltation to the right hand of the Father. However, the New Testament does not leave it there but presents us with a tableau that puts us inescapably into the picture and "on the spot." In Acts 1:6–11 the brief but dramatic story of the ascension sets up the "eschatological tension" which creates the Church as we know it. The term "eschatological tension" refers to that sense of urgency, or of task or mission, that thrusts the followers of Jesus out of the seclusion and peace of the victory that Jesus has already won for them into the labors and suffering and insecurities of the quest for the full realization of the reign of God in the human community which has not yet been attained.

The setting of the ascension story should be carefully read and meditated. Luke has referred briefly to the ecstatically happy experiences of the disciples who were together with Jesus for forty days in which he showed himself to them alive after his passion and instructed and encouraged them, telling them to wait in Jerusalem for the baptism of the Spirit to come upon them. Their immediate response is the startlingly unsuitable one of asking him whether this, then, is the time that he will "restore the kingdom to Israel." This seems to imply that they still held a very impoverished and restricted view of the redemption or liberation he had brought by his death and resurrection. It seems that they were thinking in terms of a narrowly conceived, possibly still military national liberation of Jews from Roman occupation. Rather than discouraging them by a direct statement of the suffering that still awaits them and of the sheer magnitude of the task, he directs them to leave the outcome to the wisdom and foreknowledge of God, but to expect great things from the power they will receive from the outpouring of the Holy Spirit, for it will make them witnesses to proclaim what they themselves have experienced far beyond the confines of Israel to the whole world of God's good creation.

It is at the conclusion of this speech that he is lifted out of their sight and separated from them by a cloud, a symbol that recalls the great "theophanies" or revelations of God in the history of Israel. Two men in white, a conventional description of "heavenly messengers" or revelatory experiences, redirect the attention of the disciples from staring into the sky to undertaking the short journey back to Jersualem and obeying the instructions left by Jesus. Acts 1:13–14 enumerates those present as the Eleven (who with the missing Judas Iscariot had been his most constant companions during his public ministry) as well as some women including the Mother of Jesus, and some other relatives of Jesus whom we do not know by name. These are the people who were all together in one room in the Pentecost story as told in Acts 2.

The most important message of the ascension scene is not really the exaltation of Jesus to the right hand of the Father because that is told also in other ways. The most important point here seems to be that they, the followers of Jesus, are left with a task, the completion of his task among their fellow human beings. As they themselves tell the story, this sets up a dilemma because they have very little idea at this point of what the task is and even less understanding of how to go about it. Everything points to the need and longing for the Pentecost event. The Spirit is to make their task clear to them and is to empower them to fulfill it. It is not explained who or what this Holy Spirit is because the theme of the Spirit of God is well known to anyone acquainted with the Scriptures and traditions of Israel.

The Spirit or wind or breath of God appears in the creation stories, hovering over the waters of chaos when the darkness still covers the abyss. God breathes his own breath or Spirit into the lifeless form of Adam, and that is how human beings come to life: by having God's own Spirit breathed into them. After sin introduces death and exile into human lives, the breathing of the Spirit of God in the world can never quite be taken for granted again. It becomes a rare and wonderful event. There is a hint of it when the waters dry after the flood in the time of Noah, and when the Red Sea is dried up before the Israelites in the flight from Egypt. There is mention of it in crucial revelatory or vocational moments in the lives of the great prophets, usually in the form of a mighty wind rushing, though in the story of Elijah it is in the form not of storm and power but of a gentle breeze stirring with the sound of silence (1 Kings 19). The Spirit is mentioned in the Gospels of the New Testament also, in connection with the conception of Jesus in Mary's womb, in the story of the temptations in the desert and in the baptism by John. In the scene of the baptism, the Spirit is hovering over the water as at the creation, and the hovering suggests the image of a dove (Lk. 3:21–22).

In the Last Supper discourse in John's Gospel, Jesus speaks much about the Spirit of truth, the Advocate, whom he will send to them from the other side of death. In telling of the actual moment of the death, John writes that Jesus "gave up his spirit" (Jn. 19:30), apparently intending the implication that it is by his death that Jesus breathes forth to his followers that Spirit of God now so rare and precious in the world, which is his Spirit by which his whole life has been lived, and which he is able to breathe into his followers only in his death. The whole meaning of the Pentecost story seems to be that they must also breathe in the Spirit and come alive with it in a new creation which draws together the fragments of the broken Adam into one body again—one body which is in a profound sense the body of the new or second Adam, the body in the world of the risen Christ. The task of the followers of Jesus then emerges as a task of gathering, assembling, in the Greek *ekklesia,* which we translate as Church. It is a task of gathering the scattered people of God into the unity of harmony, of worship of God, of concern for the common good, of mutual service in the generosity of self-forgetfulness of Jesus Christ. The task that Jesus necessarily had to leave undone was the task of their response to his self-gift with their own. He laid the foundations and made the beginning, and he poured out his own Spirit in death for them to make it possible for them to respond. But the free response must still come from them, and they in turn must give themselves first in order to make it possible for others who have not known Jesus in the flesh to make their response.

The Pentecost scene itself though brief is full of allusive imagery which speaks eloquently of the task of the followers of Jesus as they understood it at that time. They heard a powerful wind which seemed to fill the whole house where they were, and they saw tongues of fire that flickered over their heads. The Spirit entered into them and filled them, and the first consequence was that they were able to speak intelligibly to speakers of strange tongues gathered in Jerusalem for the feast. The scene is reminiscent of the story of the tower of Babel. In that story people were building a tower to make themselves the equals of God and then lost the power to communicate with one another. In this story the disciples were gathered in an upper room in a posture of humility before God, and by the gift of the Spirit the ability to communicate with one another is restored to them.

The Spirit or breath that has entered into them gives them a communion with God himself even more intimate than they had by being in the fellowship of Jesus. Now the gift of the divine presence that Jesus brought to them has really become internal to them. That seems to be the meaning of the symbol of fire which has always represented God and the sheer exigence of the all-consuming love of God. Jesus had said to his followers that he had come to bring purifying fire to the earth and was longing with his whole being for that fire to be kindled. The Pentecost gift as the outcome of his passion and death seems to embody the fulfillment of his desire. The tongues of fire descending and resting upon them seem to testify to a radical transformation of their hearts and lives.

The first expression of this transformation is in their going out to others to proclaim the good news of the death and resurrection of Jesus Christ and the outpouring of the promised

Spirit of God. They call for repentance, the Greek *metanoia* which is a change of heart, consciousness, personal orientation, and the Hebrew *teshuvah* which is the turning, the turning back to God. They also invite their listeners to be baptized in the name of Jesus Christ so that their sins may be forgiven and they may receive in their turn the outpouring of the Holy Spirit.

If the reader should wonder what is involved practically speaking in being baptized and forgiven and living by the Spirit, these questions are answered briefly but very explicitly in the following verses (Acts 2:42–47). They formed a community by their fidelity to the apostolic teachings (reshaping their understanding of the hope of Israel in the light of Jesus), by their brotherhood (which included the holding of goods in common and the diligent care of the needy as well as their common purpose to do and suffer anything in order to restore creation in Jesus Christ), by the "breaking of bread" (which meant the Eucharist celebrated in homes for all who could gather) and by praying together constantly in praise, thanksgiving, petition and repentance. They also continued at that time to worship in the temple and to engage their fellow Jews in conversation about the fulfillment of the hopes of Israel whenever the opportunity offered.

A number of dimensions and polarities emerge in the understanding of the task and the community that we came to call "Church." It exists because the work of Jesus is incomplete. Therefore it exists in an interim time—the time between the definitive breakthrough that Jesus made by his life, death and resurrection in the past and the full realization of the reign of God in the human community in the future. That means that the Church is essentially a movement within the human race—a movement toward reconciliation with God and toward community among ourselves, the two aspects being essentially inseparable. This in turn means that the Church exists not for itself but for the benefit of the whole human race and for the sake of the goal which is the reign of God. This understanding explains the explosive missionary thrust of the Church in the earliest generations, the urgency behind Paul's missionary journeys, the early and difficult decisions to go to the Gentiles as well as the scattered Jews, and the precipitous founding of new local churches with a variety of leadership patterns. In fact, in those earliest generations, the followers of Jesus expected the end and consummation of history with the public triumph of Christ to come within their own lifetimes.

While on the one hand the Church has always seen itself as existing for the sake of bringing about the reign of God for all the human race, yet on the other hand its focus was always inward as well as outward and forward. The means for striving toward the coming of the reign of God was basically the transformation of the human vision, of human goals and behavior and most particularly the transformation from human selfishness (echoing Lucifer's "*non serviam*") to authentic worship and community life for others and for a common purpose (echoing Christ's "not my will but thine"). The sobering realization behind much of the life and practice and organization of the Church since the early days is this: the only way to reform the world and the affairs of men in their true human dimensions is by what one does with one's own style of life and relationships, and this is precisely what Jesus did. For this reason the work of Jesus was bound to be incomplete; he gave himself and his teaching and example in his whole life but finally had to give himself in his death and pass on the responsibility of transformation in the Spirit of God to others. They in turn could follow or imitate him by what they were, what they taught, the example they gave and the relationships they built with others which supported those others in a personal conversion. In the end many of those first disciples consummated their self-gift to others in the service of God by dying a martyr's death as Jesus did.

The vision that underlies this is a vision in which the continuing task of the Church in the world is the continuing conversion of persons and of structures of society from the original "sin of Adam" and the cumulative entanglements of sin that have shaped human history and society. Because that original sin is seen as a declaration of uncreaturely independence (in disobedience to God the Creator and in disregard of the rights and needs and claims to freedom of fellow creatures), therefore the whole task of redemption is seen as one of conversion or turning that inclines the creature to seek persistently among the confusing and distracting claims of a sinful world for the sound of the authoritative voice of God and inclines persons and communities to renounce self-assertiveness and bend themselves to serve the needs of others. Jesus made a beginning in this at the center of the human enterprise simply because he lived totally by the Spirit of God and in personal trust and dependence on the Father, and therefore was so strongly rooted that he could turn the whole tide of history singlehanded. But few people, even in their spiritual maturity, are able to do this without the support of reciprocity within a community. The task of the Church in relation to its own members is to be such a community of reciprocity of service and self-surrender.

Related to this is another polarity in the existence of the community called Church. In one sense it is and must be a community of the redeemed. It must give "eschatological witness," that is, it must offer some experience now in history of the enjoyment of the reign of God. Such testimony or experience can only be offered by a community which is already wholly surrendered to God, living totally by faith, hope and love, fully at peace within itself and utterly undaunted by threats of persecution, disruption or seduction from without. In such a community, its leaders and those in authority must be servants of the community and its members, seeking neither status nor power nor any other advantage for themselves, humble in quest of the truth by listening always for the voice of God without regard to the status of the human speaker who may utter it. In such a community all must seek what is best for the common good, not for their individual or partisan advantage. All must contribute whatever they can and claim only what they really need. Yet, clearly, the Church that must be and do all these things is made up of sinful individuals, themselves warped by their experiences of the sinful structures and values and expectations of the world, themselves in the painful and laborious process of personal conversion. The Church is forever trying to give its glorious witness of the reign of God and to carry on its task of conversion of the world through the medium of individuals and Church structures that are plainly only partially converted themselves.

Since earliest times the question has been raised whether this can indeed be done. The only possible answer is that with God all things are possible, though humanly this is an unreasonable hope. Christians see the "divine element" in the Church in the Father who founds it in creation itself and calls and beckons it through history toward the end-time, and in the Son who launched it by that gift of himself which turned the tide of history, and in the Holy Spirit which is the true life and soul of this complex and highly problematic venture in the world of human affairs. On the basis of this understanding, Christians have maintained since patristic times that no matter what the scandals, disappointments, betrayals and schisms which the Church may suffer, it cannot in the end fail to attain its God-given purpose, though (as later Christian humor added) God may have to "write straight on crooked lines."

This fundamental conviction is expressed in Christian piety by the role given to Mary the Mother of Jesus. From earliest times Mary has typified the perfected Church of the end-time. When Christians have asked themselves whether it is really possible that the redemption should be completed in the world by people themselves so unredeemed as yet, the veneration of the immaculate conception or total sinlessness of Mary, attributed to the foreseen merits of her Son, was a symbolic answer to that question. This doctrine of the immaculate conception was a way of saying that through Jesus God has brought about a new and untainted creation, his bride Mary or his bride the Church, uncontaminated by the leaven of past evil, a special and merciful intervention of God. Similarly, when Christians asked themselves whether the heavenly goal was really attainable, the answer was expressed in the veneration of the assumption of Mary into heaven, "body and soul," to be reunited to Christ her Son, a symbol of hope and reassurance to the whole struggling Church which she represents. This had already been foreshadowed in the Book of Revelation of the New Testament in the vision of the portent in heaven, the woman clothed with the sun, crowned with twelve stars and having the moon under her feet (Rv. 12:1–17). Probably written originally about the people Israel as mother of the Messiah, this passage was soon applied both to Mary and to the Church, because these both bring forth the Messiah into the world in a struggle with the forces of evil.

Mary is not only held up as a symbol of hope for the Church as a whole but also as a model of obedience to God's call and of self-effacement for individual Christians. There does not seem to be any sex-role determination intended here. She is held up as a model for Christians both male and female. Just as it is not intended that only men should imitate the self-gift of Jesus that is enshrined for us in the Eucharist, so it is clearly not intended that only women should imitate the self-effacement of Mary that is enshrined in the symbolism of Marian devotion. However, there can be no doubt that Mary is not proposed as a model for "assertiveness training" but precisely for self-effacement in service to others, and herein lies an inescapable conflict of values between the traditional teachings of Christian faith concerning what is liberating and salvific (or healing) and the tenets of contemporary Western culture on that theme.

Mary is also proposed, to the scandal of some, as a mediatrix with Jesus and through him with the Father, so that in Catholic tradition Christians are encouraged to pray to her. This custom of intercession by an intermediary is one with which we are familiar in human affairs even in our avowedly classless society. One does not have access directly to the president of the country or to the ambassador of another country or even to one's own dentist. Traditionally Christians have learned from the human Jesus and the apostolic preaching and ministry to think of communion with God in terms of human mediation. This applies not only to Jesus and Mary and the apostles but was extended in the course of the ages first and in a special way to martyrs of the faith, who were not only remembered, honoured and imitated but were asked before and after their deaths for their intercession with God on behalf of their fellow Christians still engaged in the struggle against evil in the world. The custom was then further extended to holy bishops and to other noteworthy followers of Jesus whose intercession was asked in prayer after their deaths.

There is an obvious sense in which the merits and prayers of the saints in the past mediate God's grace for the community in the present. What they have already done necessarily benefits future generations because it establishes trust, healthy relationships, sound shared values, good structures, helpful expectations and so forth. What seems to trouble people today, faithful Catholics not excepted, is an uneasy sense that perhaps to "speak with" the saints who have died in our prayers is nothing but an exercise in fantasy in which we are in the truth of the matter talking to ourselves in the shape of a projected partner in dialogue.

This problem may be due to a too literal understanding of what is happening when we "talk with" God in prayer (a topic to be futher discussed in Part IV of this volume). When we pray to God, we may indeed be speaking words silently in our minds or vocally, but this is because it is our ordinary human way of projecting ourselves to another. God's way of receiving our prayer is shrouded in mystery. We suppose it to be bound neither by time nor by space nor yet by the limits of language, nor in the least strained by the call for attention from many voices at the same time. God's way of answering our prayer is also quite other than in the pattern of a conversation between two human partners. In fact, "conversation" is an analogous way of thinking and speaking about prayer, and this analogy can be applied to the relationship between the living and those who have already died, leaving the matter at rest in the realistic acknowledgement that it is in a realm in which we neither know nor can express in strictly appropriate terms the reality in which we participate.

The tension between the Church as a community of the redeemed and the Church as a community of sinners is also expressed in the Catholic custom of praying for the "repose" of the dead. Again the assumption is made that there can be a real and effective communication between the living and the dead and that there can be a kind of gift of good deeds (redemptive living) and intercessory prayers from those yet living to those who have died with the project of their own turning to God in self-surrender and to others in service as yet incomplete. Again, there is an obvious sense in which no one finds a problem with this. Most people who die leave all kinds of work and all kinds of relationships unfinished. It is a task of mercy, charity, filial piety, community spirit and perhaps even of justice to complete the unfinished tasks of those who have died. The contemporary problem seems to be with the question whether such completion of tasks including works of piety and repentance and prayers for forgiveness can possibly affect the outcome for the person who has died. That it can affect the success of the projects or the welfare of the surviving family and so on is clear. Catholic faith and teaching holds that such exchange and communication between the living and the dead is effective, though it makes no attempt to say how or to try to decipher the indecipherable.

This whole vision of interdependence has been named in Christian tradition by the term "communion of saints." The term as we have it in the ancient creeds was probably originally intended to denote the communion or sharing of the "holy things," that is, the mysteries of the followers of Jesus, the sacramental celebrations and the Scriptures and teachings, but in the course of time it has come to be understood rather as a communion or sharing among the holy people, that is, among all those past and present who have entered into the life of the Spirit by baptism into the community of Jesus.

The inner strength of that bond of life in the Spirit is expressed not only in praying to the saints for their intercession and praying for those who have died for forgiveness and final fulfillment, but it is also expressed by intercessory prayer for one another among the living. This has raised similar questions in our own times about the actual value or effect of such intercessory prayer for others. Clearly, changed behavior and attitudes on the part of any member of a community in some way affects all other members; therefore a minimal claim for prayer on behalf of others is certainly that those who practice it make life easier and the environment more supportive for those others indirectly by becoming more converted to God themselves. Catholic faith and teaching suggests something more than this. It suggests that the analogy by which we extend the human custom of appealing on behalf of others to our relations with the transcendent God as known through Jesus Christ is an analogy that will not lead us astray. Although we cannot know in appropriate terms how God acts, we can know with assurance that God is not less merciful or faithful than human persons, and we can therefore use analogies from human relationships accordingly. This follows logically from the characteristic insistence of

Jesus himself that the most appropriate analogy for thinking about and relating to the transcendent God is expressed by a familiar and affectionate term for father.

However, there is another way yet that the tension between the Church as Church of the redeemed and as Church of sinners is expressed in the traditional patterns of life and organization in the community of the followers of Jesus. Because it was so clear from earliest days that most of us most of the time do not really live up to the ideals that we profess, an elaborate teaching was developed around the "evangelical counsels" of the New Testament. These counsels of the Gospels or counsels arising out of the "good news" of the nearness of the reign of God are sayings of Jesus in which he recommended what was not unconditionally demanded of everyone. They included, for instance, meekness to the point of total non-violence and heroic vulnerability, perpetual prayer, radical renunciations to avoid temptation, and so forth. In the course of time, two of these counsels of Jesus recorded in the Gospels came to be rather central in the traditional teaching. These were virginity, the renunciation of marriage and a family of one's own for the sake of total personal dedication to the coming reign of God, and poverty in imitation of Jesus, the renunciation of ownership and exclusive use of property with the status and security that this always offers. Those who followed such a way of life in celibacy and poverty, whether as missioners and wandering preachers, or as servants of the needy, or as hermits dedicated to a life of prayer and penance, were acknowledged as holding a special place in the community and keeping alive for the community the "eschatological witness."

In the course of time such people found for practical reasons that they needed guidance in their way of life and that when they lived and worked in groups there had to be some authority and order. This could have remained a purely practical expedient but it did not. Out of their practice they recognized that their attitude to authority and guidance had spiritual and redemptive aspects. The attitude of Jesus in the sayings "I do always the will of him who sent me" and "Not my will but thine be done" was interpreted as another evangelical counsel, sanctioning vowed obedience to one whose authority was guaranteed by the Church. The ideal in this vowed obedience is that of a kind of tour de force in the conversion or turning from self-will and self-assertion to a total surrender and commitment to the will of God. It is seen therefore as being at the very heart of the work of redemption—a bond which paradoxically sets people free to set one foot, so to speak, already within the reign of God that is yet to come, because having surrendered private and competitive goals in their lives they are wholly able to pursue the common goal of the redemption wherever and in whatsoever way they are needed.

This, of course, has been institutionalized in the vowed religious life of religious orders and congregations officially approved by hierarchic Church authority, which has given such communities the special task of maintaining the "eschatological witness" in the Church as well as sustaining much of its apostolic labors. However, it would be a great error to suppose that thereby two levels of membership are established in the body of Christ which is the Church—one which is mainly passive, allowing people to draw the benefits of what Jesus did and suffered, and demanding of them only observance of the commandments, and another level of membership which is active, asking people to share with Jesus in working and suffering for the redemption and therefore demanding of them observance of certain evangelical counsels. There are no such two levels of membership recognized in Catholic tradition. All are called to active membership, participating in the redemptive work and suffering of Jesus and observing not only the commandments but the counsels according to each one's vocation.

This idea of individual and different vocations within the

body of Christ is as old as the letters of Paul who uses the analogy of the different functions of different organs of a natural body (1 Cor. 12:12–30). There are several important attitudes implicit in it. It suggests great caution in judging the sincerity or generosity of other Christians, because all are not called to the same service, though all are called to serve. It also implies a personal stance of prayerful attention in order to discern God's call to oneself. In the Pauline text cited above, it is assumed that the vocation to a particular ministry may come directly from Jesus (as with the apostles) or directly from the Spirit (as in the case of special charismatic gifts) or indirectly from both of these by way of a Church appointment. By the second century of Christian history we can see from documents such as the *Didache* (containing an oral catechesis and a Church order for the conduct of initiation, Eucharist, and local church affairs) that tension between the charismatic element in vocations and the element of Church appointment or institutional guarantee was already strong.

This tension between communion in the Spirit in spontaneity and simplicity on the one hand and institutional strength and stability on the other has surfaced repeatedly in the course of history but is particularly strong in our times. This is in itself neither surprising nor shocking because it is a conflict built into all human social activity, and it is particularly so in the Church which is the movement of peoples toward the reign of God and therefore can never be satisfied with any established order although it is nevertheless heavily dependent on an established order in the life, worship, teaching and outward thrust of the community. That is why the Catholic Church has not only a permanent structure of sacramental celebrations and an ordained priesthood but also a hierarchic governmental structure, a code and tradition of canon law, and an official teaching channel (known as the *magisterium*) for the scrutiny and formulation of orthodoxy in Christian beliefs.

In some respects the hierarchy has through the ages institutionalized its own opposition and rendered its prophets respectable by officially recognizing the religious orders and
congregations and certain lay movements. But this process can
never be exhaustive. The Spirit of God which is the Spirit of Jesus alive and moving in the Church cannot be harnessed and
continues to burst forth like leaping flames in unexpected
places. In some respects also, the *magisterium* has institutionalized its own opposition by recognition of pontifical universities
and institutes, of diocesan and other seminaries, and (though
less rigorously) by the acknowledgement of other Catholic universities and colleges. This guarantees a certain tension because
scholarly investigation of sources will sooner or later raise questions about some commonly held assumptions and interpretations and because scholarly reflection will sooner or later
suggest alternative approaches, formulations, and solutions to
problems. This scholarly intervention in tradition will not be the
only voice to be raised, for the voice of experience of the ordinary faithful of the community and particularly of those who are
suffering in any given situation is also the voice of the members
of the body of Christ and therefore in some sense the Spirit
making itself heard in the Church.

In the Catholic tradition, however, when all voices have
spoken, the last word goes to the *magisterium* of the hierarchy,
and this is a cause of wonderment to some and of scandal to others both inside and outside the community. Strangely enough,
this appears as scandalous for the same fundamental reason that
causes scandal over the role assigned to Mary and the saints,
namely, that it seems to deny the immediacy and spontaneity of
God's grace and Spirit in the lives of believers. However, two aspects of our human situation must be remembered. First of all,
in the order of creation human beings are necessarily corporeal,
existing bodily in space and time and interdependent for sustenance and survival, and they are also social or necessarily rela-

tional, shaping their language, thought, convictions and values and expectations by their relationships and interdependency with others. Secondly, in the order of history, which is an order of sin and redemption, the task and necessity of relation to others acquires a certain poignancy and urgency from the fact that the prototypical sin is the "*non serviam*" of Lucifer, the stance of self-assertion that refuses to bend to others.

It is in the first place this refusal to accept situated or limited freedom as a community freedom held jointly with others that causes the garden of delight at the heart of creation to disintegrate into disparate and hostile elements. Therefore, at the very core of the task of redemption is the need to recapture the realization and acceptance of the principle that the will of God, to which human beings as creatures must be wholly oriented, is ordinarily and necessarily mediated by other human persons in all their frailty and shortsightedness and sinfulness. Not only is social order and structure with patterns of authority a practical necessity in the order of creation, but a certain arbitrary use of authority in a bullying manner with oppressive sanctions and unreasonable determinations is guaranteed by our situation within a history of redemption from pervasive consequences of past sin.

This is the understanding behind the assertion that the death of Jesus is redemptive and behind the special veneration of the martyrs and confessors of the faith (these last being those who have suffered for their faith but have not actually been killed for it). This is also the understanding behind Christian respect for civil authority qualified only by the absolute claims of obedience to God, whether civil authority is exercised by believers or unbelievers, graciously or harshly. But most especially this is the understanding behind the religious respect and obedience which Catholics traditionally give to those who hold authority in the Church, whether it be authority to interpret moral obligations, authority to command observances and religious behavior, or authority to determine orthodoxy in the professions of faith and their elaboration in catecheses and theology.

Much in the patterns of Christian life and religious practices and in the formulation of beliefs and their explanations is ultimately arbitrary. There are various possible and good ways of arranging and organizing. The one element that is not arbitrary in the work of the redemption in which the Christian community is engaged is the need for unity and peace of hearts and minds and wholehearted commitment to the common endeavor with others. In order that such unity and peace of hearts and minds may be achieved, the one essential and indispensable element of asceticism (that is, of discipline and struggle) is the renunciation of the self-willed stance that asserts independence of control and direction by others. This is why Church authority has such an aura of spiritual significance in Catholic tradition. The vow of obedience taken by religious is different in the extent and detail and explicitness of its application; however, it is otherwise not discontinuous with the ordinary obedience of the Christian in the Church but rather typifies the latter.

In spite of the above, obedience to Church authority is not always simple and obvious but may be a matter of careful reflection and judgment. It is not intended as a childish attitude of abstaining from the use of personal intelligence and judgment. From the inevitable dependence of childhood one moves into the use of one's own faculties with a certain degree, often an exaggerated degree, of independence. The Catholic ideal of obedience to Church authority is not that the individual should regress from this stage of growth but that there should be a further movement forward to greater maturity in which people are able to make a genuine community commitment. This means a serious intellectual, critical and personal effort to understand the goals, ideals, and traditions of the community and a realistic assessment of the strengths and weaknesses, the possibilities and limitations of the Church and its membership and leadership as they actually are in their sinful, provisional, historical existence. Such is the basis for that creative collaboration which obedience is intended to be in the Catholic tradition. Because the tradition is a living tradition in history (a history of struggle between sinful and redemptive forces) it is always still in process of formation and adaptation, and that process cannot be without differences of opinion and experience and therefore cannot be without conflicts. This is no cause for alarm as long as it is without bitterness and hatred.

It is in this context that patterns of leadership have developed and shaped themselves in the course of the centuries. In the earliest churches there was the general authority of the apostles and their teaching and the local authority of Church leaders, individuals or collegial groups, who might have been selected and appointed by an apostle or might have emerged by popular consent because of evident leadership qualities. Soon all local churches came to be under the leadership of single overseers known as bishops, and important matters came to be referred to local synods or councils of bishops. From the legitimation and subsequent establishment of the Church in the Byzantine Empire of the fourth and subsequent centuries arose the custom of assembling all the bishops or representatives of local churches scattered through the known world. It was understood that where a consensus of the representatives of the local churches was reached, there the very Spirit of God had spoken in the Church and the matter was binding on all Christians.

Increasingly in ancient times, and decisively after the medieval schism of Eastern and Western churches, the local churches of the West came to see in the patriarch of the West, the bishop of Rome, considered the successor of the apostles Peter and Paul in his office, not only a ceremonial leadership but the authority to make on his own initiative the kinds of determinations that the councils had made. This did not happen without great struggles through the centuries over the issue of centralization of authority and initiative. It became a central issue in the further schism of north and south in the Western churches at the time of the sixteenth-century Protestant Reformation. It became an issue again in the remaining Roman Catholic communion of churches in the latter half of the nineteenth century at the First Vatican Council.

The First Vatican Council proclaimed that when acting within clearly and rather narrowly prescribed limits, solemnly and officially for the benefit of the whole Church defining doctrine (specifying teaching) to be held by the whole Church on matters of faith and morals (that is, interpreting the teaching of the Gospel), the bishop of Rome, known as the Pope, possesses the infallibility which Jesus intended the Church to have in such matters. The practical effect of this is that such teachings become in themselves permanent or unchangeable in the same way as the teachings of the great councils of the Church. The First Vatican Council also made broader statements about the supreme authority of the Pope in the government of the Church, but it is this statement of "infallibility" of teaching that most frequently causes bewilderment and distress. It has actually only been explicitly invoked on two occasions, in the definition of the immaculate conception of Mary and in that of her assumption, both doctrines explained earlier in this chapter and both defined in defense of the traditional piety of ordinary Christians against slick arguments of the sophisticated.

The practical dilemmas and difficulties of ordinary Catholics in their struggle to give wholehearted but intelligent and responsible obedience and allegiance to the Church have not been with these pronouncements of the "extraordinary *magisterium*" in solemn official definitions but with the "ordinary *magisterium*" of Church teachings, particularly in the areas of morality, as carried on not only by the Pope in person but by various officials and commissions of the Holy See, by episcopal conferences and by local chancery offices. In these matters the standard guiding principle of Catholic tradition is that it is a matter of loyalty and sincerity to form one's conscience (one's habit of making practical moral decisions in particular situations) by acquainting oneself as well as possible with the Church teaching and the reasoning behind it, by seeking sound and competent advice, and by prayer and making every effort to attain detachment (the desire simply to do what is best in the situation, or at least to do what is not sinful). All this being done, however, the Catholic tradition soberly and uniformly holds that in the final step the individual must follow his or her own conscience (that is, practical judgment of what is right to do in this particular situation).

Related Material

Some books on the Church that may be helpful are listed here. The document Lumen Gentium *of Vatican II is available in English translation from the USCC or in the collection made by Walter Abbott,* The Documents of Vatican II *(America Press). A commentary on this document issued on behalf of the United States Bishops' Conference entitled* The Church in Our Day *is also available from the USCC. A significant encyclical of Pope Paul VI on the topic,* Ecclesiam Suam, *is available in English, entitled* His Church *(Our Sunday Visitor Press). There is a helpful reflection on the meaning and implications of the Vatican II document by Avery Dulles,* The Dimensions of the Church *(Newman/ Paulist). A later book by Avery Dulles,* Models of the Church *(Doubleday) explores the different ways that people may think about the Church in terms of biblical models.*

A small essay on the Church as communion is The Open Circle *by Josef Ratzinger (Sheed & Ward). Extending this idea in terms of evangelization is* The Church as Mission *by Eugene Hillman (Herder/Seabury). A longer and largely historical study on the same topic is* Do We Need the Church? *by Richard McBrien (Harper & Row). Another very strongly historical study is* The Idea of the Church *by B.C. Butler.*

8

The Fragrance of the Spirit in the Sacraments

What most surely holds together the experience of Church as communion and that of Church as institution is sacramental celebration. The idea of sacrament, as already mentioned in Part I of this book, is basic in the Christian understanding of human relationship with God. The experience and the notion are older than the word that names them (and is borrowed from secular usage). Sacrament is embodiment. Human persons cannot meet or experience God except as embodied. The chosen people Israel, with its holy land and its holy law, its sabbath observance and its great festival celebrations, was such an embodiment from early times, offering its mediation in Scripture and tradition even to Jesus himself.

For Christians, the fundamental sacrament or embodiment of God's presence and merciful power in the world is the person of Jesus. The creation story tells us that the human person as such is made to be the image of God and therefore the embodiment of the divine presence in the world, and that the human person as such is given life by having the very breath or Spirit of God with which to breathe. The whole sorry saga of sin tells us that the image of God in the human person is denied and distorted by the determination to attend to oneself alone so that the embodiment of God is obscured and ambiguous. By the self-centered stance that is sin, the human person refuses to breathe with the breath or Spirit of God and thereby fails to breathe forth the Spirit into the world to and for others. In the human Jesus the image of God is recreated in the world. In him the Spirit of God breathes in the midst of the human community and is breathed forth into others.

This is why the hymn at the beginning of the Letter to the Ephesians tells of the mystery of God's purpose revealed in Christ in whom all things are reintegrated and reunited with God (Eph. 1:3–14). In him the presence of God in the world becomes tangible and visible again, because his personal stance of being wholly for God and for others liberates the merciful power of God as the source and sustenance of human freedom. The risen Christ draws others into the sphere of his own freedom, and it is in the experience of their own growing freedom to be for God and others, to be happy in self-forgetfulness, to be content to be interdependent in pursuit of a common purpose in life, that the followers of Jesus become in their turn part of the mystery, the sacrament or embodiment of God in the world. They become members of the body of Christ which is the Church or gathering of God's people, the new Adam or new creation. They embody or give tangible presence in the world to the risen Christ who embodies the transcendent God, the Father.

Thus, because Jesus Christ is seen as the fundamental sacrament of God's presence in the world, the communion of the followers of Jesus is the second level sacrament. But that union of the followers with Jesus and with one another must of course be tangibly, experientially, corporeally expressed. It is not an embodiment until it is embodied. Such embodiment in a broad and diffused sense should take place in the whole life and activity of the community and in all its structures, but it has a much sharper focus in the ritual gathering for worship that we call the Eucharist. At the third level the mystery of God is revealed in human experience in the celebration of the Eucharist, the central sacrament in the sacramental system of specific celebrations which the Catholic Church cherishes and traces back to the earliest times.

The Christian Eucharist has a pre-history in the traditions of Israel. Jews, from ancient times to our own days, have been commemorating the exodus from Egypt in the Passover seder. This is a ritual meal, an action-meditation, elaborated from the ordinary table grace, which recalls the liberation from the slavery in Egypt as the wonderful intervention of God in history to show himself as the powerful and compassionate One and to call his people to himself as witnesses to the whole world (including themselves). They are to witness to the lordship of God by the quality of their lives and their peoplehood. Hence the importance of the law and the observances and the significance of the land. In the Passover seder ritual elements are laid out on the table and consumed with readings, meditation and commentary, singing of psalms and hymns, and festivity. It takes place in families, but because of the common calendar and the common elements of observance it binds together the people both in the present generation in all lands and across the ages. It affirms and constitutes their peoplehood.

The New Testament attributes the Christian Eucharist to the creativity of Jesus himself in adapting the Passover ritual and infusing it with new meaning, the meaning of unity in him in the new exodus from death to a sinful world to the resurrection in a new creation that is focused Godward. The accounts of the Last Supper or farewell meal that Jesus took with his disciples before his arrest and execution are highly stylized and certainly contain speeches that are composite accounts of the teachings of Jesus from various occasions. We have these accounts in 1 Corinthians 11:17–27, Mark 14:22–25, Matthew 26:26–29, and Luke 22:7–20. (The Gospel according to John does not give a parallel account but it does offer two separate commentaries on the event, one in chapter 6 and the other in chapters 13–17.)

The common core in these accounts is their situating the action of Jesus within the Passover seder tradition and their isolating the blessing over the unleavened bread and over the fourth and last cup of wine. They show Jesus breaking and sharing the unleavened bread, which is the bread of affliction and also the bread of the breakthrough into the radically new life of freedom and peoplehood. In breaking it and giving it to them, he says: "Take and eat, for this is my body." It has generally been assumed that this was intended to mean, "This bread is my body," and that the task of interpretation was concerned with what is meant by equating the two. Scholars have, however, suggested that it more probably was intended to mean that this action of blessing, breaking, sharing and eating in such an assembly in his name and memory was to be seen as the embodiment of the presence and Spirit and power of Jesus in the community. Certainly this seems to be the way Paul understood it in the passage from 1 Corinthians cited above. Paul accuses the Corinthians of "not recognizing the body" when they have factions, exclude some people and embarrass the poor among them, eating and drinking to excess while others go hungry, when they are gathered for the Lord's supper. Not recognizing the body in this context seems to be concerned with the embodiment of the risen Christ in the celebration which is also the welding of individuals and groups into one community.

The common theme in the blessing of the fourth and last cup of the Passover seder as adapted by Jesus is the saying, "This cup is the new covenant in my blood" (1 Cor. 11:25), or "This is my blood, the blood of the covenant, which is to be poured out for multitudes for the forgiveness of sins" (Mt. 26:28). This links the ritual meal directly with the passion and death of Jesus, so that Paul can speak of the celebration of the Eucharist as celebrating the death of the Lord until he comes (1 Cor. 11:26). It also interprets the passion and death of Jesus as a self-gift to others as sustenance. That is why Paul can conclude that to enact the Eucharist and share in the Lord's body and blood (his gift of himself) while at the same time refusing to meet the needy of the community with the gift of oneself and one's resources is to participate in the Eucharist unworthily, missing the point and showing deep disrespect for the self-gift of Jesus in his passion and death.

This is the Eucharist of Christians, which constitutes them the embodiment of Jesus in the world and demands of them a far-reaching surrender of selfishness and self-centeredness to become a community which supports each individual within it by a life in the Spirit which creates a new world, a new realm of grace, and a reciprocity of conversion to others. Because the Eucharist constitutes the followers of Jesus into such a community it also makes them a witness people to the world at large, with a missionary thrust outward to draw others into transformed relationships, expectations and structures that move toward the welcoming of the reign of God. This is why the ancient hymn found in the second-century document known as the *Didache*— a hymn sometimes sung at the liturgy today—can pray for the Church of God to be gathered in from the four winds, that is, from the whole world. This, also, is why the *Dogmatic Constitution on the Church* of Vatican II can say that even if the Church does not include all people and looks at times like a rather small number, it nevertheless is a seed of unity and hope and salvation for the whole human community (n. 9). But for this the Eucharist must be more than ritual, more than a Sunday morning obligation. It must be the summit or climax of Church life to which all is ordered and from which everything flows (*Constitution on the*

Sacred Liturgy, n. 10). In other words, the Eucharist properly understood really shapes and transforms the community in all its activities, its values and its expectations.

In the course of the centuries, the celebration of the Eucharist has become surrounded with many standard traditional prayers and preceded by a general and inclusive community confession of sin and repentance, and a series of Scripture readings with meditative passages interspersed and, ideally, a homily explaining the Scripture readings and discussing their application to the life of the present community. This, of course, was necessary precisely to make sure that the action of the Eucharist would not remain simply a ritual but would become the source of a pervasive change in the community. For this reason, the readings, meditative prayers and homily were considered an integral part and not simply an adornment. We have a long history of an established cycle of readings as well as a treasury of commentary and homilies on them that dates from the patristic era.

As the Church of the West moved its center of gravity northward among the barbarian peoples in the early Middle Ages, unfortunately much of this treasury became inaccessible and the whole living sense of the meaning of the Eucharist became dim not only for many of the people brought in by mass (and sometimes forced) conversions, but also for most of the priests who were poorly educated and appointed to benefices (incomes that went with the performance of pastoral duties) by landowners who had built the churches and endowed them. These clerics did not have a seminary formation and were not chosen for their piety or their knowledge of doctrine. As may well be imagined under such circumstances, superstitions were rampant, magical practices were not unknown, and the religious professionals made what profit they could out of their benefices.

Under these circumstances questions arose that had not troubled the communities of the patristic age. Charles the Bald, one of the successors to the throne of Charlemagne in the ninth century, addressed a question to certain theologians in monasteries that had maintained some of the ancient texts and oral traditions. He wanted to know what was meant when the celebrating priest said the words "This is my body"—whether that should be taken in some figurative sense or literally, and, if the latter, how that could be explained. The philosophical and linguistic and ethnological sophistication of these monks was not great. That is to say, they were not aware of the variety of cultural idioms and imagery and uses of language to the same extent that we are, nor did they have the analytical ability and training that the ancient Greeks had enjoyed in philosophical discussions, nor yet did they have a sense of history that would enable them to put the Gospel sayings of Jesus in the context of ancient Israel and its culture and language and literature. These monks did the best they could, but it led to centuries of controversy which do not seem to have been particularly helpful in fostering the faith and redemptive transformation of the society.

The argument over the proper formulation of what happened to the bread and wine in the Eucharist continued into the Protestant Reformation of the sixteenth century. The answer offered in the eleventh century by a scholar named Berengarius that the change was of a symbolic nature was not acceptable at that time because that seemed to most knowledgeable persons to involve a denial that Jesus was really present in the Eucharist. The Church approved at the Fourth Lateran Council in 1215 and continued later to maintain against Protestant opposition that the word "transubstantiation" appropriately describes what happens and is the orthodox word in the Catholic tradition. The Fourth Lateran Council did not intend this word in a technical philosophical sense as a reference to Aristotle, though it was later so understood by many with much resulting confusion. It intended to express the conviction that in the eucharistic celebration the bread and wine that are shared and consumed become for the community the reality of the presence of Jesus and of communion with him. The word acquired a technical meaning as a theological term (that is, a word representing an impenetrable mystery) which was different from the technical meaning as a philosophical term (that is, a word expressing a particular conceptual analysis of physical beings). When contemporary theologians suggested terms that might have more readily available meaning to modern believers—"transfinalization" or the transformation of the purpose that constitutes the reality of bread and wine, and "transignification" or the transformation of the meaning that constitutes the reality of these things—Pope Paul VI in an encyclical letter *Mysterium fidei* insisted on the continuing use of the older term because so much Catholic piety is entwined with it.

Meanwhile the real problem with the centuries-old debate is that by focusing so much attention on what happened to the bread and wine it took the attention away from the strictly spiritual and far more important question of what ought to be happening to the community, and in what ways it was expected to change and by what power and motivation. This is why the contemporary theologies and the teachings of the Second Vatican Council, especially in the *Constitution on the Sacred Liturgy* (officially known as *Sacrosanctum concilium*), focuses rather on the presence of Jesus to the congregation in the Eucharist than on what happens to the bread and wine. It points to the presence of Jesus in the word of Scripture that is read, in the faith of the community that is gathered to participate, and in the action and things used which are the outreach of Jesus himself who initiated this celebration and reaches across the centuries and across space and culture change in this action to touch his followers in the most intimate communion.

This last aspect, that the presence of Jesus to transform his followers by his own life and Spirit (that is, by the life of grace) is due to the initiative of Jesus himself to which the Church's actions are but the response, is a very old claim in the history of the Church. It came under explicit scrutiny in the early fifth century, and St. Augustine of Hippo wrote about it. The question arose concerning the position of the faithful who discovered that those who had baptized them or presided over their eucharistic celebrations were themselves schismatic, heretical or scandalous in their lives. Some people had anxieties as to whether their baptism under those circumstances had really brought them into the Church of Jesus and whether they had been participating in real Eucharists or only in an empty show. In response to this, St. Augustine gave an answer which the Catholic Church has officially endorsed ever since. The sacraments are actions not of any individual but of the Church as such, not only the community gathered on a particular occasion but the community that makes up the Church of Christ through the ages. The sacraments are, in fact, actions of the Church in which the community extends the action of Jesus himself. Therefore they are properly considered actions of Jesus himself, and they are effective simply by virtue of what is done, which means by virtue of Jesus Christ in his Church as the doer of the action. That makes the outcome independent of the merits of a particular minister who may be presiding over the celebration, because he is not properly the one responsible for the action but only the deputy. This does not mean, however, that the Catholic Church attributes magical power to the sacraments; they cannot establish a recipient in grace if that person does not undergo a profound, progressive, lasting conversion in all aspects of life.

This concern with conversion in all aspects of life is expressed by the celebration of a number of other sacraments which are in one way or another dependent on and closely related to the Eucharist. In the New Testament itself one can really only distinguish two sacraments, baptism and the Eucharist, though the activity of the apostles, missionaries, elders and deacons includes other actions of a sacramental character in a broader sense (actions in which human persons collaborate in constructing occasions of encounter with God by using material elements with sacred associations). Protestants since the sixteenth century have contested the Catholic teaching concerning seven sacraments. This teaching grew out of Church tradition and was shaped quite slowly. The patristic Church left us testimonies concerning "the mysteries" which seem to have included both the rituals and the teachings of Christianity. There was at that time no concern with numbering the mysteries; attention was focused on keeping them secret from prying eyes of outsiders who might treat them with disrespect, on understanding them precisely as mysteries (whose truth could not be exhausted by human understanding), and on participating in them worthily with great fidelity to the tradition.

It was only in the Scholastic theology of the Western Church of the Middle Ages that the question of the numbering of the sacraments came up. There seems at first to have been more agreement that there were seven than there was agreement on what the seven were. That, however, is because seven is a symbolic number signifying plenitude, in this case meaning more particularly that the sacramental activity of the Church covered all aspects and phases of human life, leaving no profane areas of existence to constitute a neutral territory between sin and salvation. The enumeration given by Peter the Lombard in the twelfth century was made official Church teaching by the Council of Florence in 1439 and defined as Catholic doctrine against the Protestants at the Council of Trent in its seventh session in 1547. Besides the Eucharist and baptism, therefore, the Catholic Church celebrates the sacraments of confirmation, penance, anointing of the sick, holy orders and matrimony.

What makes it important to distinguish these as sacraments is the claim made for them, as discussed above, namely that they are the actions of Jesus Christ himself and effective as such. This claim is based on the assertion made repeatedly in the official teaching of the Catholic Church that the whole treasury of sacramental activity has its source in the person of Jesus, in spite of the fact that we can indeed trace the historical evolution of the rites and the theological explanations of them as we have them now. In enumerating seven sacraments the Church also makes the claim that in these celebrations grace is dispensed, as it were, in two ways. There is the establishment or restoration or growth of the life of the Spirit in the general sense called "habitual grace" or "sanctifying grace" (to be discussed in the following chapter), and there is also the specific "sacramental grace," that is, the effect or outcome that is indicated by the symbolism of the sacrament itself.

The initiation of new members into the community is in three stages, dating from the earliest centuries. These are baptism, confirmation and first full participation in the Eucharist. Baptism symbolizes a going down into the waters of destruction in union with the death of Jesus and a rising to new life out of those waters. In other words, it is a baptism into the death and resurrection of Jesus Christ in order to become a member of the community that embodies his risen presence in the world. The ancient practice was, of course, to baptize adults who had lived either as Jews or as pagans. In course of time a lengthy catechumenate was developed, sometimes lasting as long as four years. This was devised to inform the candidates but also to form them as followers of Jesus in their whole life style and orientation and to test them as to their firmness of purpose and their perseverance in it. The baptism itself was therefore a final and decisive step on the part of the candidates and on the part of the community for which long preparations had been made. It constituted a commitment on both sides—a commitment from the candidates to live a Christian life as members of the community which they had chosen in freedom and maturity, and a commitment from the community to accept them as members and to give them the support that would mediate grace in their lives.

In these circumstances the confirmation of that baptism by the bishop's imposition of hands on the heads of the candidates followed immediately, because there was no reason to delay it. From there they were led to their first full participation in the Eucharist, because it was the first time they were really qualified to offer the sacrifice of Christ and the Church in Christ's name.

In the baptism of infants that became the more general practice of the Church in subsequent ages, the order is different, so that some important distinctions must be made concerning the significance and effect of these steps. When an infant is baptized, the child itself makes no commitment, though the community makes its commitment to the child to provide it with a Christian, redemptive environment in which to grow up and shape a vision of life, values, goals, and patterns of behavior. That means that the catechumenate in this case follows the baptism which must be considered a tentative step made on behalf of the child by others. But that also means that the child in the course of religious instruction must be treated in some ways as a guest being invited to make an assent of faith and to become a member. The child cannot properly be treated as a committed member being held accountable for a commitment already assumed. This follows from the nature of faith, for authentic faith is a radical personal commitment made in personal freedom and maturity. This, of course, is reason enough for the historical development that separated confirmation from baptism by a span of years.

Confirmation traditionally is the sacrament of Christian maturity. That is to say, it is the acknowledgement by the bishop on behalf of the Church community that an individual is ready to be considered a full-fledged member of the community, undertaking its responsibilities and able to join with the community personally in offering the sacrifice of the Eucharist. However, while it therefore recognizes officially the outpouring of the Spirit of Jesus in the life and actions of the individual, the sacrament of confirmation is also a prayer and blessing that calls for a further bestowal of the gifts and fruits of the Spirit in the life of that person. This is the specific sacramental grace to which the symbolism of the sacrament points.

In all the discussion of the life of the Church so far, it has been taken for granted that there is an ordained ministry within which people are commissioned and empowered to celebrate the sacraments and to undertake other pastoral duties within the community. It has also been taken for granted that this ordained ministry is integrated into a hierarchy that governs the affairs of the community as to beliefs, organization and moral codes. Jesus certainly instituted a chosen and appointed ministry in the community that he left to continue his work, though the particular shape of that ministry and the assignment of tasks within it has changed constantly and developed extensively in the course of the ages, as have the conditions for ordination to those tasks. As mentioned earlier, the tension between charismatic ministries and ordained (that is, officially appointed) ministries began more or less with the beginning of the Church itself. There seems to have been some sort of crisis in the second Christian century. In the document called the *Didache* there is a plea to the congregations to treat celebrants of the Eucharist sent to them by the bishop with the same respect they accord to those who celebrate simply because all recognize that they have the charisms for such leadership in gathering the communities for worship. This implies a certain ascendancy of the charismatic leadership in the minds of the faithful generally, and the document does not condemn it. Yet by the end of the second century there seems to have been a more or less universal rule that only those designated by the bishop should preside over the celebration of the Eucharist. In any case, the bishop himself was clearly envisaged as the most appropriate, even as the ordinary, celebrant, with others filling his role in "extraordinary" circumstances.

With the growth and establishment of the Church in large geographical areas, a standard pattern of ministry divided the ministers into three main categories: bishops, presbyters and deacons. Their functions became more clearly defined and were quite extensive, until eventually they included not only sacramental and instructional ministries, but also a great deal of administration of temporal affairs. The elaborate power and responsibility assumed in the Western Church in the Middle Ages, and kept in some instances into modern times, included exercise of territorial sovereignty by the Popes, exercise of judicial authority and control of inheritance laws and customs by Church bodies, powers of taxation by bishops and others, and so on. Gradually the exercise of these more secular functions came to be recognized as a hindrance rather than a help in the discharge of ecclesiastical ordained ministries. As the secularization of the modern world continued to strip away such powers from Church officials, theologians reflecting on the meaning of the sacrament of holy orders did not mourn the passing of this temporal glory. Increasing plurality of religious affiliation in modern societies is still further eroding the privileged status that goes with the ranks of the clergy and therefore raising important questions about the essential elements of the ordained ministry and the effects of the sacrament that places a person within that ordained ministry.

Although Catholic teaching and theology refers to one sacrament of holy orders, ordination might very well have been listed as several sacraments, because it consists of several distinct phases that ordain a person to distinct ministries. There are some preliminary steps leading to subdiaconate, but the first phase of ordination that is in practice today also a permanent ministry is that of the diaconate. The role of the permanent deacon, as recently re-established in the Catholic Church, includes the ministries of baptizing, preaching and instructing, visiting the sick and seeing to the needs of the poor. Actually, all of the ministries are also sometimes performed by lay Christians, but the deacon is charged with them as his special calling. The role of the priest is more specifically concerned with the sacramental ministry, and in particular with that of presiding at the eucharistic celebration, administering the sacrament of penance or reconciliation, and anointing the sick.

The role of the bishops is seen in Catholic tradition as one of succession to the apostles, though it is certainly not the same foundational role. In the early centuries the bishop was seen especially as the symbol and means of unity both in the local church and among the local churches, and in this the bishop and the Eucharist were always mentioned in the same breath. This task of unity makes them the bridge-builders of tradition across the generations as well as the architects of order and harmony in the present. For these reasons the special ministries connected with episcopal consecration are the confirmation of Christians, the ordination of priests and deacons, and the consecration of other bishops, as well as the ministry of "overseeing" the life and activities of the Church from which the term bishop (*episkopos*) is taken.

The special sacramental grace envisaged by the symbolism of the sacrament of holy orders is a particular bestowal of the Holy Spirit which empowers the candidate to fulfill the tasks of this ministry in the name of Jesus and as Jesus would do it. Ever since the fifth century it has also been maintained that this sacrament, like baptism and confirmation in the Church, seals or "marks" the person with a characterization that is permanent and is not lost, even should the individual be relieved of the discharge of priestly functions or obligations. In other words, to be aggregated to the ministry of Christ in this specialized way within the Church community is seen as radically affecting the very identity of an individual thus called, chosen and ordained.

The sacrament of matrimony would seem at first sight to be ill-assorted among the other sacramental mysteries celebrated in the Catholic Church. They all appear to belong in the realm of sacred activities while the sacrament of matrimony seems to belong squarely in the secular realm. They all seem to be concerned with Church functions, while marriage seems to be concerned with quite definitely temporal and worldly functions. And yet the realization that a truly Christian marriage is a sacrament that mediates into the here and now the mystery of Christ's love for and union with his Church is already given in the thought of Paul in the New Testament (Eph. 5:25–33). He in turn is very much in continuity with Jewish thought on the matter which has marriage as a sacrament (though without the use of that term) of the creative love of God in the human community. Of course, marriages commonly fall far short of that in the reality of a sinful history. But when a marriage is truly celebrated in Christ, when therefore the Spirit of Jesus breathes in the relationship, the apparently impossible is realized and the redemption is being accomplished precisely in the everyday patterns of the secular realm. The marriage is a sacrament because the reality of the union is in Christ, not because it is celebrated by a ceremony in the Church. Yet the ceremony in the Church, as with a confirmation, has a double function; it acknowledges the breath of the Spirit in the union of Christians, but it also is a prayer and a blessing for a full realization of the gift of the Spirit.

The experience of the Church has always been one of struggle and is expected to continue in that way with failures and setbacks. In the earliest ages Christians certainly recognized that after baptism they still had a path of further conversion ahead of them, and they expressed this in various ways, such as reconciliations in the community before the celebration of Eucharist. The reconciliation of sinners with the Church in an official celebration was rare, invoked in situations of great scandal in the community, and apparently offered only once in a lifetime in the early centuries. There is a long and complicated history of the way that the public reconciliation of spectacular sinners and the private repentance of all Christians in their continuing struggle with habits and situations of sin came to be fused into a single pattern of sacramental celebration always administered by an ordained priest specifically designated (given "faculties") by the bishop of the local diocese. What is important in that long story is the growing realization that any attempt to divide Christians into sinners and saints, or into the faithful and the scandalous, is hypocritical, for all are in some measure sinners and all in some measure scandalous in falling short of the wholehearted and unconditional following of Christ.

The sacrament of penance, cause of much doubt and confusion among Catholics today, is not only an important specific difference in the Catholic Church among the Protestant communions. It is also, together with the Eucharist, the constant and principal means that releases in the community of the followers of Jesus "the fragrance of the Spirit" (an expression taken from the fourth-century Church Father, Cyril of Jerusalem, when speaking of repentance, conversion and transformation in Christ). The sacrament of penance is that celebration of encounter with Christ in the Church whose specific purpose and grace is to mediate a continuing personal and particular conversion to Christ. Its meaning is intimately related to the seriousness with which Catholic tradition recognizes the reality of original sin as pervasive in values, structures and expectations of society and therefore deeply rooted in the values, goals, attitudes, habits, inclinations and self-image of individuals.

This pervasive reality of sin makes the Christian life conflictual and gives it a radical counter-cultural quality that is arduous and difficult to maintain. It is all too easy for Christians to deceive themselves about where they stand in relation to Christ's redemptive work in the world. The Catholic teaching, therefore, is that the virtue of penance has a central place in the lives of even the most faithful of Christians, and that its practice has an "interior" and "exterior" aspect. The interior aspect consists of the turning of one's mind and heart (that is, of one's attention, imagination and thoughts, and of one's desires, affections and decisions) away from everything that is selfish, self-centered, motivated by fear, pettiness, greed or ambition, turning them toward God in gratitude and self-surrender. The exterior aspect consists of an exigent process of change of life-style, personal behavior and relationships so that they will authentically express the interior turning or conversion. So exigent is this that the tradition guides Catholics into going further than the simple correction of what is wrong by self-denial in legitimate matters, or by undertaking laborious or painful experiences that are not strictly necessary. In fact, the Church has even canonized as saints (that is, held up for admiration and imitation) some Christians of the past who went to extravagant lengths in this direction.

This is particularly the understanding behind the seasonal observance of Lent as a time of penance. Historically the Lenten observance aggregates all Christians to the ranks of the public penitents who were singled out conspicuously in the early Church. Historically the sacrament of penance is particularly associated with the season of Lent as a preparation for entering fully into the paschal mystery, that is, into personal participation in the redemptive work of Jesus in his death and resurrection. In a lesser way, the season of Advent (in preparation for Christmas and Epiphany) and the days between the feast of the Ascension and that of Pentecost have the same sense of a time of repentance in preparation for entering into the mystery of the redemption. It is for this reason that the revived rite of communal penance celebrations tends to take place especially at these times. In a communal penance celebration, people define themselves as penitents (that is, as persons in need of conversion and earnestly seeking it) simply by being there. Further than this, they have the visible and tangible support of a community bent on the same purpose. The communal penance celebration also offers the occasion for a preacher to attempt to discern and expose sinful aspects in the contemporary culture that people are less likely to recognize as such. This gives participants the opportunity and challenge to examine their consciences on matters that would not otherwise occur to them and to confess the failures thus revealed either to a priest-confessor present at the communal celebration for that purpose, or on another occasion, or specifically to God and generically in an act of contrition made with the whole community at the communal celebration.

In spite of the reinstitution of a rite in which general absolution is given to a whole community in response to a generic confession of sin and contrition, hierarchic authority in the Catholic Church has been slow and reluctant to allow this to take the place of individual and specific confession of sin to a priest-confessor. Although such was not the practice of the earliest Church, this pattern of the sacrament of penance grew out of Christian experience and reflection upon it, and the Church came to appreciate its value so highly that it has been loath to let it fall into desuetude in a time of rapid cultural change in which large numbers of Catholics seriously question the practice.

One may hazard some conjecture as to why the official guidance of the Church favors the continuance of individual sacramental confession. Few people are able to be as perseveringly exigent with themselves as true Christian conversion requires unless they are explicitly and specifically accountable to another person. In any case, people are seldom if ever good judges in their own cause. The discernments one needs to make about one's own temperament, character, dispositions and values, in order to see the need of conversion concretely and enter into an appropriate strategy, are certainly best made under the guidance of a wise and appropriately learned person. Besides this, the beginning of conversion is certainly to humble oneself by the acknowledgement of sin. This can be done in utter privacy to God alone in one's own conscience, but that tends to be rather ethereal and vague when it does not culminate in an oral confession specific enough to be understood by another human person. Finally, if the prototypical sin, as depicted in the story of Lucifer, is precisely an inauthentic assertion of independence, there is an inherent logic in close dependence on the mediation of another in conversion to God.

All this, however, could equally well be an argument for confession of sin to any other (lay) Christian who is serious about the Christian life and has a gift for discernment. In fact, historically such lay confession and spiritual guidance was at various times rather widely practiced. The element that is added when the confession is made to a priest licensed (given "faculties") by the local bishop is the characteristically Catholic element of submission to institutional authority in the Church. To make a full confession of sin and sorrow for sin, ask for absolution in the name of the Church and accept a work of penance imposed (no matter how nominal that usually is in the contemporary Church) is a personal stance of obedience to God as mediated by Christ in the Church. It is a very practical embodiment of the relationship to God in repentance. It may be said further that to confess in some detail to a regular confessor (that is, regularly the same one) and to take his guidance seriously is the principal way in which lay persons can make an effort to put their lives more extensively under obedience to Christ in the sacramentality of the Church.

Associated rather closely with the sacrament of penance in the history of the Church is the anointing of the sick. This sacrament mediates the grace of Christ's redemptive passion and death and resurrection at a time when it is most urgently needed. It mediates this grace by the rallying of the Church to the support of the sick through the minister of the sacrament and the representatives of the community. Underlying this practice is the assumption that in time of serious sickness there is the most temptation to depression, discouragement, self-centeredness, impatience and general collapse of focus and values. It also assumes that in serious sickness where there is danger of death, loss of control and independence, and some inevitable isolation and loneliness, there is a special moment of summons to enter more deeply into the mystery of Christ's death and resurrection as the mystery of the return of all things to God. The purpose of this sacrament is to turn such moments into occasions of growth and grace.

Related Material

On the sense of sacramental mediation of the human relationship to God as we have inherited it from the traditions of the Jews, some Catholic readers have found the writings of A. J. Heschel full of revelatory insights, particularly The Earth Is the Lord's *and* The Sabbath *(both published by Harper & Row). Other helpful books by Heschel which are somewhat longer are* Between God and Man *(Free Press) and* God in Search of Man *(Harper & Row). Also provocative in offering insights from other traditions on the aspects of Catholic tradition that our modern Western civilization has tended to obscure is Raimundo Panikkar,* Worship and Secular Man *(Orbis Press). At a more sophisticated technical level, some readers may find help in understanding the contemporary problems and possibilities in sacramental worship in the* Concilium *volume,* Revelation and Experience, *edited by E. Schillebeeckx and B. van Iersel (Seabury).*

A classic meditative approach to the Catholic practice and understanding of the sacraments from the patristic era is Cyril of Jerusalem, The Mystagogical Catecheses, *available in several series of the Fathers of the Church in translation. There is a vast contemporary literature on the liturgical and doctrinal aspects of the sacraments. Inspirational and regulatory Church documents as well as good commentaries on them are available from The Liturgical Conference, Washington, D.C. The most important of these documents for our times is* Sacrosanctum Concilium, *the* Constitution on the Sacred Liturgy *of Vatican II, available, for instance, in Walter Abbott,* The Documents of Vatican II *(America Press).*

An historical approach to the understanding of sacramental symbolism is offered in Liturgical Piety *by Louis Bouyer,* The Bible and the Liturgy *by Jean Daniélou,* The Primitive Liturgy *by Josef Jungmann, and* The Prayer Life of the Church *by Bonifaas Luyckx (all from Notre Dame University Press).*

9

Newness of Life
in the Gift of the Spirit

In previous chapters the word "grace" has been used frequently. It represents a characteristically Christian understanding of the relationship of God to human persons in history. Throughout the Hebrew Scriptures (the Old Testament) the point is made that God constantly shows his love, his favor, his fidelity to his sinful and utterly unworthy people. This is expressed in many stories and images and is traced back to the creation story in which God quickens Adam with his own breath or Spirit and invites Adam and Eve to walk in his gracious company in the cool of the evening. The suggestion is that of an overabundance of kindness and condescension—of something far beyond what is due, far beyond what could possibly have been expected. In fact, in the story about Moses at prayer (Ex. 33), Moses is to know when God has "passed" in any situation by the resonance of the great names of God which are undeserved mercy and undreamed-of compassion. The most constant images of God that are presented in the Hebrew Scriptures are those of a parent and of a lover, the untiring parent of a wayward child and the reckless lover of the unfaithful beloved. If the parent is stern it is out of unrelenting creative love for the child, and if the lover is exigent it is to rescue the beloved from disaster.

In the Gospels of the New Testament Jesus is presented as the gracious and utterly unmerited gift of God to his people—Jesus who breathes the very Spirit of God in their midst and who in turn breathes that Spirit forth to them as an utterly unmerited gift that he makes to his people, his followers, his Church. In the writings of Paul in the New Testament this gift-quality, this gratuitousness of Jesus and the Holy Spirit, gradually develops into a rather specialized use of the Greek word (*charis*) which we translate as "grace." Paul is particularly concerned to emphasize the gratuity of God's saving power exercised in our behalf in the person and life, death and resurrection of Jesus. He wants to emphasize that it is not something that had been earned by observance of the law of Moses or by any other good works. Paul seems to use the word in blessings when he wishes his converts the grace and peace of our Lord Jesus Christ, in exhortations when he describes what a community is like that is living according to the good news of Jesus Christ, and in prayers of thanksgiving when he refers to the gift received in Christ. Using another vocabulary, Paul speaks of the change that happens in communities and individuals when they are converted to Christ as "justification" or becoming holy. This idea was later assimilated into the notion of "grace."

As the Church traditions took over these themes from the Scriptures, grace came to mean both the gift of God and the quality (or qualitative change) in the human person receiving that gift. This is to be expected because the gift of God is precisely the change in the receiver. In the course of time, the gift of God that we call grace came to be acknowledged as really identical with the Holy Spirit, the self-communication of God, God as immanent (or dwelling within the community and the individual). Thomas Aquinas in the thirteenth century could write that we are using different language here when we are speaking about God's action upon creatures and when we are speaking about the effect within creation of that action, but that the reality of which we speak is the same. In other words, all the discussion about grace is still a discussion of the quickening of the human person and the human community by the very breath, or Spirit, or life of God himself. It is this which inspired in the traditions of the Eastern churches the theme of sanctification as the "divinization" of human persons. In this way of thinking, the divine Word became what we are in Jesus in order to make us what he is, that is, to share divine life with us.

This lovely imagery and language could become altogether ethereal and elusive if it were not specified in some extremely concrete terms. The stories about the Spirit of God in the Hebrew Scriptures and also in the New Testament do this and Paul sums it up succinctly. He writes that "the harvest of the Spirit" (in earlier translations and in traditional Catholic literature more frequently rendered as the "fruits of the Spirit") is "love, joy, peace, patience, kindness, goodness, fidelity, gentleness and self-control" (Gal. 5:22). This is practical enough as a set of criteria by which to judge the extent to which a community or person lives in the grace of God, that is, by the Holy Spirit. Lest it not be clear enough, Paul also gives a description of behavior that results from sinful nature that resists the Spirit, namely "fornication, impurity and indecency; idolatry and sorcery; quarrels, a contentious temper, envy, fits of rage, selfish ambitions, dissensions, party intrigues and jealousies; drinking bouts, orgies and the like" (Gal. 5:19–21). Elsewhere Paul adds to his "harvest of the Spirit" compassion and humility (Col. 3:12).

In the First Letter to the Corinthians, chapters 12–14, Paul considers the "gifts" of the Spirit at great length, including wise speech and ecstatic utterances, healing and wonderful powers, prophecy and discernment of spirits (1 Cor. 12:4–11). Christian tradition later developed the various listings of gifts of the Spirit into one standard list that became the basis of much commentary in the various texts and schools of spirituality. This list made the gifts of the Spirit seven, that being the number of fullness or perfection, and these seven are: wisdom, understanding, counsel, fortitude, knowledge, piety and fear of the Lord. These came to be given quite technical meanings. However, tradition followed Paul closely in a further observation, namely that the truly important and central qualities of the life of the Spirit (the life of grace) are faith, hope and love (known in later tradition as the "theological virtues" because they relate directly to God) and that the crucial test is in love (1 Cor. 13:13). Again, Paul makes that test very explicit by describing loving persons. Such people are patient and kind. They are not envious, boastful, conceited, rude, selfish or easily offended. They do not bear grudges or assume superiority over others because of their sins. They seek the truth fearlessly and are indomitable in what they will undertake and endure (1 Cor. 13:4–7). It is scarcely possible to be more explicit or more exigent than this.

The term "faith" has developed in Catholic theology to designate something rather narrower than it does in the New Testament—a matter that has caused difficulties and misunderstanding between Protestants and Catholics. When Protestants speak of salvation by faith alone, faith has for them the broad New Testament sense of acceptance of Jesus as Lord and Savior and full self-disclosure of God. This acceptance is a total personal response. When Catholics speak of the theological virtue of faith they more usually refer to an analysis of what is involved in that total personal response in which the word "faith" stands for one aspect. That aspect is the intellectual or cognitive. By faith in this sense, one opens up one's perception, imagination, and understanding to the truth of God revealing himself. One allows God's revelation to shape one's vision of reality. One receives this revelation with an open mind as it is given in the person of Jesus Christ and through the mediation of the Church.

The term "hope" is less problematic because it has never been used in quite such a comprehensive sense as faith. The theological virtue of hope is the reaching out of the will and all the striving of a person to God as the future fulfillment of human existence both communal and individual. It implies confident expectation based on the fidelity of God and also on the sincerity of the desire which subordinates all other objectives to it and guarantees corresponding efforts. The emphasis in Christian hope in the earliest centuries was more on the outcome for the community than for the individual. That is why the appropriate efforts in the Christian life were seen as having to do with community relationships and structures. With the establishment of Christianity, structures were taken more for granted as they stood and hope focused more on the outcome for the individual beyond death. With the disestablishment of the churches in modern times since the Enlightenment, Christian hope for the world and its salvation seemed to disappear entirely into the individual hope as religion became very much a private affair that had to be kept out of public decisions and policies. In the contemporary world, both among Protestants and among Catholics, the public dimension of Christian hope is coming to the fore as a crucial determinant of the new life in the Spirit, that is, the life of grace. But this is happening with considerable tension and conflict because many Christians today are accustomed to the idea that religious commitment does not have anything to do with the political sphere.

The theological virtue of love, or charity, is the whole core of life in the Spirit, as mentioned above. In the biblical perspective as interpreted by Jesus this love has two inseparable dimensions—total self-surrender to God and attachment to his will, and universal, undiscriminating, selfless service of others. They are inseparable because to love God and accept one's creature-liness is to fit into one's place and gladly, peacefully welcome others in theirs. In the order of history, which is an order of sin and redemption from sin, this is necessarily a stance of self-sacrifice because, given the sinful structures, values and expectations that prevail, people are not "in their places." Most of us most of the time are doing some trespassing and are surreptitiously trying to focus our world not toward God and the realization of his purpose but toward some private project of our own. This is why Christians see the pagan project of moral virtues practiced out of shared self-interest as an impossible one, and claim instead that it is only by the healing gift of God, bestowing on us his own Spirit and life, that a good and integrated human existence becomes possible. The moral virtues, such as sobriety, courage, industry, modesty, fair play and so forth (collected in pagan thought under the headings of prudence, justice, fortitude and temperance), do indeed play a most important role in the redemption as evidenced by Paul's lists and admonitions, but Christians see these good behavior pat terns as flowing from the gift of God as a consequence of the theological virtues of faith, hope and charity which are constituent elements of the gift of grace which is the outpouring of the Spirit of God.

In spite of these convictions, Christians through the ages have suffered from a certain temptation to self-sufficiency, which is nothing other than a disguised and very respectable-looking return of the sin of Lucifer and the sin of Adam. In the history of Christian theology this was played out quite dramatically in the fifth century beginning with an exchange of statements of position and objections between St. Augustine of Hippo and the monk known as Pelagius. Their followers kept the debate going for a long time and the issue has never really died in the Christian community. Augustine was overwhelmed with the hopelessness of the human situation as depicted above.

Concretely he was looking at the corruption and disintegration of the late Roman Empire under attack of the barbarians from without and morally and civilly rather close to collapse within. Augustine looked at the world as he knew it and looked back over his own dissolute life before his Christian conversion and did not hesitate to speak of the human race as a "doomed mass" of human misery. No sort of effort, no matter how heroic, could possibly rescue the human community or the human individual from disaster. Of themselves human beings could do absolutely nothing good or wholesome. Only the special intervention of the healing grace of God, offered out of his totally undeserved and gratuitous compassion, is able to rescue human persons from total disaster. Such is the understanding of Augustine, and from his writings one has the impression that he thinks few indeed are in fact rescued.

The monk Pelagius seems to have been appalled by what he heard and read of Augustine's teaching because he judged that it simply added fuel to the prevailing immorality and despair. He thought that by asserting grace in this way Augustine was in effect denying human freedom and therefore also human moral responsibility. The main interest of Pelagius and his followers seems to have been in the preaching of a moral revival; therefore he stressed each person's individual freedom as the key gift of God, accompanied by the revelation of God's law and the example of Christ. Thus far, he was really just continuing the Pauline and traditional teaching with a different emphasis from that of Augustine. However, he went further and denied the general state of corruption and inclination to evil which the tradition even then saw as consequent upon "the sin of Adam." For Pelagius, the concept of original sin seems to have been reduced to the force of bad example. He claimed that the grace of God was offered equally to all and consisted of the elements already mentioned above, namely the freedom of the will, the revelation of God's law, and the example of Christ. With these aids, he concluded, people can live sinlessly if they set their minds and wills to the task in lifelong effort without shirking or relaxing.

There is no doubt that both Augustine and Pelagius were earnest, radically committed Christians. At one level one might see the whole dispute as one between persons of disparate temperament and disposition. The Church has always had members whose attraction was more to mysticism as the fundamental mode of relationship to God and others whose attraction was predominantly to asceticism. In other words there are people who relate to God (and to other human persons) more affectively, impulsively, by appreciation, wonder and receptivity and (so to speak) more in the realm of being. Others relate to God and fellow human beings more rationally, consistently, by performance, disciplined effort and active service and therefore more obviously in the realm of doings and achievements. This tension, of course, is not only between persons but within persons, and in itself it is fruitful. Even the bitter controversy that followed between the disciples of Pelagius (who took his positions to greater extremes) and Augustine and some of his followers proved to be of immense benefit to subsequent Christian tradition because it forced a clarification of issues.

The key issues that emerged were the question of the relationship between God's grace and human freedom both in an initial conversion and in the living of the life of grace, the nature and universality of the effects of the "sin of Adam," and the compatibility of God's foreknowledge and salvific decrees with human responsibility and moral accountability. The Church answered these questions through its official teaching in ways that left some of the intrinsic tension that is inescapable in the living reality. The basic position in answer to the first question is that God always acts first anticipating any human move. This is a rather general theme of the Hebrew Scriptures, and in his first letter in the New Testament, John underscores it with his insistence that the love of God really consists in the experience that he has first loved us so that his love has taken root in our lives (1 Jn. 4:7–12). But God's gift is received by and within human freedom so that the love must be reciprocated by human effort even within the Spirit. One might put it another way and say that the grace of God activates human freedom or raises it to a greater intensity, empowering a response beyond the natural capacity of the human person.

As to the second question, concerning the effects of the "sin of Adam," the official Church teaching on original sin was already discussed in Part I of this volume. The third question continued to plague Christians in future centuries. The official Catholic answer to it is that God desires the salvation of all human beings and predestines no one to evil despite the "foreknowledge" that we must logically attribute to God once we speak about him on the analogy of human experience and action in time.

Meanwhile, the medieval teaching on grace made a point of some importance for the practical life of Christians by distinguishing two uses of the word "grace." It means not only the state of being that is the indwelling of the Spirit, the living by the Spirit, but also expresses the momentary divine promptings, inspirations, encouragements, which stimulate, support and draw to fulfillment any good deed. The practical import of this is to encourage Christians to pray constantly, to try to live so as to be open to promptings of the Spirit, and to face life cheerfully with great hope relying on the power of God. This counterbalances those ascetical traditions that encourage people to build up good habits by repeated acts which facilitate the exercise of virtue and strengthen the will. It maintains the old and necessary tension between the receptivity of the mystical approach and the discipline of the ascetical approach. The issue came to the fore in this shape in the Protestant Reformation in the question as to whether Christian believers can, and are required to, cooperate in their own conversion and redemption. In the faith and good works controversy, Catholics understood Luther and his followers to say that there could not be a thorough and personal transformation in Christ, but that there could only be the gesture of throwing oneself on the mercy of Christ by faith in him as Savior in response to which human sinfulness would be "covered over" and forgiven. The Catholic position on this is that vigorous effort is not a denial but an acceptance of total dependence on God's grace.

One further issue arose in modern times that is of present significance to all believers. Catholic teaching over the centuries had consistently rejected such manifestations of enthusiasm as resulted in people claiming they were saved because they could "feel it." However, the other extreme also became a problem— namely, grace was sometimes spoken and written about in such a fashion that there would apparently be no way in which one could tell from experience and observation whether any person (even oneself) were living in the grace of Christ or not. The life of grace, often referred to as the "supernatural life" or the "realm of the supernatural," seemed to be floating in an independent sphere, untouched by "nature" and making no impact upon, or transformation of, ordinary relationships and social structures and behavior. Clearly this was not grace as Paul wrote about it nor redemption as envisaged in the early ages of the Church's first fervor. Consequently, two contemporary theologians, Henri de Lubac and Karl Rahner, quite independently of each other, explored the whole tradition again to show that while grace is not directly related to feelings, it is nevertheless indirectly accessible to experience by the transformations in human life and behavior that it brings about. Grace works within the nature and the freedom of the human person, not somehow alongside of it or above it.

Related Material

The biblical background of this topic is rather helpfully discussed by various authors in Sin, Salvation and the Spirit, *edited by Daniel Durken (Liturgical Press). An excellent selection of primary sources on the doctrine of grace in different ages of the Church's history has been made by Edmund Fortman in* The Theology of Man and Grace *(Bruce). A good, concise contemporary discussion of grace is offered in* The Experience and Language of Grace *by Roger Haight (Paulist Press).*

The Catholic Church has a vast heritage of writings on spirituality, that is, on prayer, repentance, the virtues and all aspects of Christian life. A good introduction to this heritage would be by way of the Spiritual Masters Series or the Classics of Western Spirituality Series (Paulist Press) which are not limited to Catholic authors but do offer the best in this tradition from various centuries and cultures.

A source of Catholic teaching on life according to the Spirit that should not be ignored is the canonization of saints. By selecting certain lives and proposing them not only for admiration but also for imitation, the Church has exercised a continuing process of discernment of the Spirit at work in the community in changing cultures and contexts throughout its history. Lives of the saints, especially those that are at pains to be historically accurate and to set the saints carefully within their own historical contexts, are a primary source for the Church's teaching on the life of the Spirit.

IV

The Mystery
of the End

10

The Kingdom of Heaven
and the World to Come

The Christian message, the good news of Jesus Christ, is certainly a message about past, present and future, but the focus is on the future. The Christian message of salvation is primarily concerned with the future because it is a message that things have to change. Not only the inner attitude of individuals but their behavior, their relationships and their situation must change. Not only the affairs of individuals but those of the world and its structures and laws and distribution of goods must change. The message is that they must change, that they can change and that they will change because the transcendent God of creation wills it, because Jesus has already turned the tide of the destructive forces by his human response in the heart of the human situation and because the Holy Spirit of God which is the Spirit of Jesus working powerfully in his followers is drawing human freedom to its fulfillment in the willing response to the rule of God.

Salvation in Christian teaching is liberation, but it is not liberation after the style of the Gnostics (already mentioned in

Chapter 2). For them, to be saved or set free meant to escape from bodiliness and historicity with all the complexity, ambiguity and responsibility that they imply. It meant to escape to the serenity, simplicity and solitude of pure spirit. Therefore, their salvation lay in a very real sense in the present. Making the proper renunciations and with the proper earnestness and purity of intention, one could slip into that other world of spirit at any time and abandon this world to its inevitable fate. Salvation for Christians is genuinely in the future because it is salvation of the world. Redemption is a liberation, a setting free, not from the world and its responsibilities and claims and burdens but rather a setting free in the world to bring it to fulfill God's purpose precisely by undertaking its responsibilities and claims and burdens. Salvation in the full sense, therefore, looks to the future redemption of the whole world of human affairs, the transformation of sinful structures, the healing of painful and harmful relationships, the repairing of human community in all its dimensions, so that all is reconciled and focused toward God as its final end.

What is meant by salvation or redemption (that is, liberation) is closely related to what is understood by sin, which constitutes the alienation or ill condition from which salvation is needed, or (using another analogy) which constitutes the captivity from which freedom is needed. As already explained in Chapter 3, sin in the biblical and Christian tradition is seen mainly as that state of human existence that is constituted by the self-centeredness and selfishness of creatures. A world of self-centered creatures is a world that has lost its center and has begun to disintegrate into confusion, suspicions, injustice and oppression, general fear and warfare. An individual who is self-centered is an individual whose focus is so badly off-center that all aspects and dimensions of human life are distorted and inauthentic to some degree and the existence of such a person is an experience of disintegration, self-contradiction, confusion and frustration of goals and plans, inability to relate transparently, trustingly, generously and completely to other persons. It tends to be an existence marked by anxiety, possessiveness, a need to dominate or manipulate other people, and undue need to achieve and excel in competition with other people. Clearly, salvation of the individual means liberation from oppressive fears, harmful desires, self-destructive tendencies. It is equally obvious that the salvation of the individual and of the society or world in which the individual's life and possibilities are shaped is really one and the same process and one and the same goal. Like the individual, the society needs to be set free from oppressive fears, self-destructive tendencies, patterns of bullying and possessiveness at the expense of others and false assertions of independence.

From these considerations it becomes quite clear why the teaching of Jesus and the constant teaching of the Church through the centuries has been that salvation is by love, and that the love of God and the love of neighbor (that is, of other people) are inseparable from each other in the practice of love. If the basic suffering, captivity, entrapment of sin is the destructive pattern by which people are locked into selfishness and self-centeredness, then liberation cannot be by escape from the world and the claims of other people, nor can it be by self-hatred. Other people are not the problem; in the plan of creation people are brought into existence in interdependence on one another to form a community of reciprocal service and love in response to God's creative and transforming summons. Nor is self-love the problem; the creation story in its description of the garden of Eden expresses the conviction that people are brought into existence to be happy and find fulfillment in their lives before God, with others, in the world that exists for them. One might almost say that self-love appears as a commandment, but that the true love of self is contingent upon the proper order of values, goals, priorities, relationships and patterns of behavior.

Paradoxically, the true love of self is not found in self-centeredness or selfishness (that is, the self-seeking that provides for oneself to the exclusion of the needs and interests of others). The true love of self is God's creative and sanctifying love for the individual appropriated by the individual in glad simplicity, in acceptance of creaturely existence among other creatures, all of which God has called good and all of which exist ultimately for God in the mystery of God's overflowing goodness.

Salvation, then, is the retrieval of this simplicity and harmony of creation in which human persons are called to transcend all the limits of space and time and particular goals and relationships in order to come to further and undreamed-of degrees of intimacy with God himself in the communion of the very life and Spirit of God that is opened to the human race through the person of Jesus. There is, therefore, a sense in which all who live the life of grace opened to them by Jesus and the Spirit are already enjoying salvation in an inchoate form. There is also a sense in which salvation from the trammels of sin cannot be complete before death, and indeed the constant teaching of the Church has been that no one can claim to be unconditionally assured of salvation while yet alive because to live in a world of sinful structures, values and expectations is to live in a state of struggle. There is a further sense in which salvation has not been fully achieved until the world is redeemed, that is, until the whole human race and the whole human project have been rescued from the destruction of self-centeredness and selfishness and restored to that harmony in which all things are focused on God as their true goal. This is surely why the hope of Christians is expressed in an ancient creedal formulation as "the life of the world to come" following the resurrection of the dead.

There is and can be no other way of speaking of the content of the Christian hope than by figures of speech suggesting analogies or by negation of some of the sufferings and evils from which people need to be liberated. The imagery that Christians have used and discernment of the evils that must be negated have come to us in a continuous line of development from Israel of ancient times. Perhaps the most continuous image is that of the reign or rule or kingship or kingdom of God, sometimes expressed in the circumlocution "kingdom (reign) of heaven" because of the reverence that made Jews reluctant to name God directly. Israel's hope was rooted and founded in two historical events above all else in the people's experience. Those two events were the exodus or deliverance out of the slavery of Egypt and the establishment of peoplehood by the espousal of the tribes to God on Mount Sinai in solemn covenant. In these two events Israel saw a great and yet unfulfilled promise of God to his people and through them to the whole human race. One of the ways that this promise was described was in terms of bringing the people into the land promised to their forefather Abraham, but it was clear that simple possession of what had been the land of Canaan did not fulfill the promise because it did not give them true peace, peoplehood and personal fulfillment for all. True peoplehood and general and individual wellbeing depended not only on the land and the material resources, but also on the law. Unless the people lived by the law given to them by God, the law in which he shared his wisdom with them, their experience of life was not so different from that of Egypt, because the rich and powerful were still oppressing the poor and weak and everyone still lived by fear—the poor by the fear of each day's routine injustices, injuries and insults, and the rich by the fear of a turn in fortune that might topple them from their privileged positions or might overturn the present unjust order of things. It would only be by truly living under the law of God that they would be the liberated people of God.

This idea cast Israel's memory back over the people's experiences of governments and kings, and they began to express their hope in terms of the reign or kingship of God. They looked back to the "golden age" when they were led by Moses and

Joshua and by a number of charismatic leaders known in the Bible as "the judges" all of whom led faithfully in the name of God and in the interests of the whole people. They also looked back to the urge for power and grandeur among the nations which they saw typified in the rule of the kings. They developed the theme that the kingship of the dynasties they had known had been a withdrawal from the true kingship or rule of God (1 Sam. 8). When God himself rules in human hearts and societies, his rule is quite different from that of human rulers and governments. They rule for their own advantage and profit and ignore the needs of the people, particularly of the poor and powerless. God, however, having no need of taxes or military service or other such levies, rules for the advantage and profit of the people and has special care of the needs of the poor and the powerless. The law of God does not need to be enforced by arbitrarily imposed sanctions of penalties such as fines, imprisonment or death. The law of God justifies itself by its intrinsic wisdom and coherence and power. The law of God justifies itself because it is the gracious gift and compassion of God that gives being and life and meaning to all.

But the rule of God and his law was always experienced as an ideal that was yet in the future. That day would come when the law of God would be written in hearts in a great renewal of the covenant in which each person's knowledge of the law of God would be immediate (Jer. 31:31–34). As the history of Israel became more and more tragic, full of conquests and dispersion by foreign powers and full of persecution of those who continued faithful to the law of Moses, the question arose more and more urgently as to when the reign of God would be realized and how it would be when it came. In the intertestamentary period (the time between the composition of the last books of the Hebrew Scriptures and lifetime of Jesus and the apostolic community) the scribes of the law taught about the coming reign or kingdom of the heavens in two ways. One was apocalyptic,

that is, it spoke of sudden and mysterious cosmic happenings
that would bring great and powerful transformations manifest-
ing that God was Lord of history. It used a language that seemed
to unveil the future in concrete terms. Lest this should be misunderstood such concrete imagery was used paradoxically, and
in great variety. At the same time the scribes taught that the only
way one could really get an idea of the reign of God that was
to come was by living now as though God and only God reigned
in the immediate society and in the world. By this means one
could, so to speak, see the coming of the kingdom of heaven
from within.

Jesus took over the imagery of the kingdom of heaven from
this tradition. He did not redefine it. We can confidently assume
this because it would have been an essential element of the
proclamation of the good news if there had been such a redef-
inition, yet none of the evangelists mention it and neither does
Paul. The teaching that Jesus took over and continued was not
about an other-worldly hope but about a this-worldly one, or
perhaps more accurately about a future-worldly one. Jesus explicitly rejected the idea that it could come by military force or
clever administration or cosmic miracles. He preached that the
kingdom of heaven was close at hand, not something reserved
for some future generation. He also declared that it was among
his listeners and within them. The Gospel according to Matthew
is full of "kingdom parables," sayings that begin: "The kingdom
of heaven is like. . . ." However, none of these offer any description of it. They seem rather to give hints as to how one might
expect the kingdom of heaven to come—gradually, almost im-
perceptibly but powerfully like leaven in dough; by way of total
commitment and radical choices, like a man selling everything
to buy the field where the treasure is buried; in the midst of the
ambiguities of history, like wheat growing all entangled with
weeds or good fish caught in the fisherman's net along with in-
edible ones; by the power of God which far surpasses all expec-

tations proportionate to human effort, as the farmer's crop grows even while the farmer sleeps and goes about his other business.

The New Testament presents Jesus as one who above all others exemplified the teaching of the intertestamentary scribes. He saw most clearly and immediately the coming of the reign of God and he saw it from within because he lived in utter simplicity as though the Father reigned in the world and no one else did. He knew more clearly than anyone the price of such a stance and from the outset was simply and unequivocally prepared to pay that price. The simplicity and wholeness of his life were a magnet and a revelation to others. To know him and be with him was evidently to have an overwhelming sense of the immediacy of the reign of God, as well as a sense of the struggle with the powers of evil and the ambiguity of the nearness of the kingdom of heaven in the context of a world whose structures and values and expectations resisted it. To be a close follower of Jesus during his public ministry was evidently to experience in oneself the tension between the reign of God accepted within oneself and bringing with it a peace and joy that nothing could shatter and the kingdom of heaven which was still a world to come in the future and was being born with great tribulation, with upheavals and conflicts in families and other groups, and with persecution not only by pagans but also by the devout. To be a close follower of Jesus was also to learn not to ask "Exactly what will it be like?" but to ask rather "What must I do to be ready for it? How can I serve the coming of the kingdom? What does the Father call me to do and to be?" To these questions Jesus was prepared to help his followers to find answers.

As the Church of the earliest ages looked back over the whole experience of Jesus, including his death and resurrection, his resurrection became for them the foretaste of salvation, of the reign of God and the world to come. This also had a pre-Christian history in Israel. In answer to the anguished question about God's apparent abandonment of his most faithful servants in times of persecution by foreign conquerors, the scribal answer had used the image of resurrection (as was mentioned in Chapter 6). Jesus endorsed the image of the resurrection of the dead as a helpful way of expressing the hope of the individual for a full share in the kingdom of heaven in the "world to come." The ambiguities and the long struggle in history for the full realization of the reign of God in the human community are not to be understood as precluding those who die in the course of that struggle. The image invoked is that of a reawakening to take part in the fulfillment yet to come, apparently in this world in a transformed order in which the harmony and joy intended in God's creation is fully restored. The imagery was further enhanced by evocation of the atmosphere of celebration of the customary eight-day wedding feast and the sense of privilege and special favor of an invitation to a royal banquet. All of this was poetic imagery not intended to be taken literally, as was the case with the Sadducees who asked Jesus about the widow who by the Levirate law had been in succession the wife of seven brothers all of whom died before her (Mt. 22:23–33).

As the Church moved further out into the world of Greek culture, Gentile Christians increasingly asked what was meant by the imagery used. Some of the earliest answers we have to this question appear in the writings of Paul, especially 1 Corinthians 15. These answers still hold, because the questions cannot be answered literally or factually so that we cannot really improve upon the way Paul answered them. As to how the dead are to be raised and what sort of bodies they are to have, Paul simply responds that these are stupid questions, that is, inappropriate questions. It is only appropriate to note that from a perishable life and body the just are to be raised to an imperishable state. It is a wonderful work of God and constitutes a victory over the destructive powers of death.

When Jewish Christians of the early Church spoke of resurrection of bodies, their emphasis was on the personal participation of the individual. Later when Gentile Christians thought of salvation in terms of the Greek idea of immortality of the soul and in terms of a timeless existence of disembodied spirits outside the world and its history, the Church found it necessary to reassert the unity of the human person and the totality of salvation by stressing the physical sense of resurrection of the body. Later teaching, however, tended to speak of the judgment and reward of the disembodied soul after death, which consisted of the immediate vision of God or the pain of loss of this immediate vision, to be followed at the end of the world (or end of history) by resumption of the risen body and a more complete experience of heavenly fulfillment or hellish loss and torment. In the course of this, the Gehenna of which Jesus spoke, which was an established metaphor for ultimate human frustration and disaster, was also interpreted and depicted in emphatically physical terms. This could only be a continuation of the figurative language of Scripture, which both Jesus and Paul had expressly said was figurative and could not be deciphered into literal, strictly appropriate terms. The sense of the Church teachings which insist on the reality of the fires of hell seems to be not that Christians must take this language as literal but that they must take it with utmost seriousness as an attempt to express something that is much greater and more significant than the language is able to encompass or the imagination to conjure forth. The general thrust of it is certainly that everything is at stake in the way human persons use their freedom.

In Catholic teaching the outcome for individuals is understood as offering more possibilities than the two alternatives of instant blissful union with God or instant final rejection. Though no warrant can be found for it directly in Scripture, Catholic teaching finds the indirect warrant in the ancient custom of prayers for the dead which goes back at least as far as the stories of the Maccabees. The teaching is that those who die with the project of their transformation in love (and in turning the focus of their lives to God) incomplete can still be purged of their remaining selfishness beyond death, or beyond human scrutiny of the end of their lives. This is really an inference from the compassion and universal salvific will of God, because it is simply unthinkable that God who is not less faithful than human persons would abandon those who lived their lives in response to his call but never managed to disentangle themselves completely from the network of sin which is selfishness. It is at the same time an inference from the realization of the ultimate exigence of God's love which calls for genuine and total conversion in all aspects of life—a project that few people seem to have finished when they die. This is the basis for the Catholic teaching about purgatory, which uses imagery constructed on an analogy with the older imagery, projecting an existence of disembodied souls outside history and outside the world in a sort of a-historical time sequence in painful purification by "fire."

Modern Christians may well wonder what they are to make of all this. Like the apocalyptic form of teaching before and at the time of Jesus, this language is only helpful if it is understood as powerfully suggestive of something we cannot in the nature of things know literally. Moreover, it is really only helpful on the same terms that the intertestamentary scribes proposed, namely, that if one lives now with a passion as though God and only God reigned in the world, one can glimpse the coming kingdom of heaven from within and thereby have a foretaste of the ultimate reality which is the content of Christian hope.

Elements of the teaching about "the last things," or the outcome of the struggle of sin and redemption in the world as seen in Christian faith, which have come more sharply into focus in our own times are the doctrines concerning the particular and general judgments. These are traditional and defined teachings of the Church which have perhaps not been given their full impact at all times in the past. The general judgment, celebrated in boldly concrete terms in Christian art and literature, is more fundamentally the thesis that all things stand under the judgment of God and that Jesus Christ is the ultimate criterion of that judgment. This includes the "principalities and powers" of the world, the political and economic structures by which people are helped or oppressed, the public affairs which seem so remote from religious values and controls but by which the personal destinies of human beings are manipulated. All this is even now under the judgment of the coming One whose standards have been made known in his life, death and resurrection. Hence there is no profane realm, no neutral territory in which Christian criteria do not apply.

The particular judgment is a doctrine that draws attention to the importance and finality of death. Because of their teachings of life beyond death, Christians are sometimes in danger of not taking death seriously but understanding it almost as an insignificant passage from one phase of existence to the next. The idea of the particular judgment is that of radical and inescapable finality. It implies that the freedom human persons have to respond to God's call and shape their lives and being by that response is a freedom in the world and in history, a freedom that lies between birth and death. The inevitability of death and judgment and the unpredictability of the timing of death place a strong exigence on the use and focus of the present moment, of the continuing present in a person's life. It is an exigence that is incompatible with simply drifting through life without ever taking responsibility for what one does with it. The doctrine of a particular judgment at death also emphasizes the mystery of human life which is not open to public scrutiny as to its ultimate destiny. It implies that the final resolution of each person's life does not lie open to observation in history.

The Christian teachings do not claim to describe "life after death," but they do imply an outcome of human lives that transcends death and history and takes place in the hidden mystery of each person's relationship to God. Any language about "life after death" is necessarily figurative and suggestive and does not convey strict information. This means that faith, hope and love must in the end be stronger than enlightened but mercenary attitudes of bargaining with God and providing security for the future. The fulfillment of the project of conversion, of a life fully turned to God as its end, is a death that is a final and complete surrender to God in unconditional trust and gratitude and in ultimate creaturely dependence, asking nothing but to return one's life to the Creator from whom it came.

Related Material

Besides those resources already mentioned in relation to the resurrection of Jesus, the following may be helpful. For the biblical background to Christian eschatology, the reader may want to turn to Rudolf Schnackenburg, God's Rule and Kingdom *(Herder/Seabury). A number of essays on the biblical and traditional development of eschatology are found in the* Concilium *volume* The Problem of Eschatology *(Paulist Press), edited by F. Schillebeeckx and B. Willems. A similar collection is that of Wolfdieter Theurer,* Readings in Christian Eschatology *(Society of St. Paul). For a brief summary of Church teachings and of contemporary theology, the reader may want to turn to* What Are They Saying About Death and Christian Hope? *by Monika Hellwig (Paulist Press) or to the eschatology section by Gregory Baum in the* American Catholic Catechism *edited by George Dyer (Seabury).*

The characteristic contemporary approach is to be found in Karl Rahner, On the Theology of Death *(Seabury) and in Ladislaus Boros,* The Mystery of Death *(Herder/Seabury). The questions raised by the social aspects of redemption are introduced in the* Concilium *volume* The Mystical and Political Dimension of the Christian Faith *(Herder/Seabury), edited by C. Geffre and G. Gutierrez.*

11

The Triune God
of Christian Faith

None of the foregoing would really make sense except in terms of the characteristic attitude of Christian faith to the mystery of God. The Christian experience of God in history confronts the limitations of human understanding with a paradox. There is no way in which that paradox can be logically resolved, though Christians have at various times attempted to do this (as will be pointed out later in this chapter). However, a claim that cannot be reduced to logical coherence is not necessarily nonsense. It may be mystery. That is to say, it may be beyond the logic of human reason rather than contrary to it. Its truth may be verified in experience, directly or indirectly. Such is the case with the Christian image of the triune being of God, which sees the ultimate horizon of reality, the fundamental ground of all being, as unity in trinity or trinity in unity, and at the same time as personal and as beyond personality, as intimately involved in history and as timeless, as immanent (or immediately present) and as transcendent (or unreachable). All these paradoxical claims are simply expressions of the human and more particularly the Christian experience of God. Most of them Christians share with Jews.

Most constant and fundamental in the traditions of Israel which Jesus shared and revered and passed on to his followers as a treasured heritage is the prayer or slogan known as the *Shema*: "Hear, O Israel, the Lord is our God, the Lord is One." This passionate faith in the unity of God has as its negative side the prohibition against idolatry which runs all through the Hebrew Scriptures and all through the Jewish tradition from ancient times into the present. It is not accidental that in the story of the temptations of Jesus in the desert, the greatest temptation (the one that claims power to deliver all kingdoms of the world into the redeeming hands of Jesus) is the temptation to worship another than the one God. It is a temptation to which Jesus responds with the reaffirmation of the one God to whom alone worship and unconditional service are appropriately directed.

This unity of God, so often and so passionately reaffirmed in the Scriptures, is not only a matter of intellectual orthodoxy, correctness of beliefs in some realm quite detached from human affairs. Faith in the one God and tribute of worship and service to that one God alone is intimately and widely influential in all human relations and all human affairs. To say that there is one God and that that God alone is to be worshiped is also to say that there is no realm whatsoever outside the dominion of that God. Neither politics nor economics, neither national interests nor international affairs, neither technology nor commerce, neither aesthetics nor productivity, can ultimately be a law unto itself. Nothing is outside the sphere of the divine exigence, the divine rule and law. Any attempt to limit religious claims, the claims of God's rule and kingship, to the private sector of human affairs is in the end again the sin of Lucifer extended in idolatries that would make some other claim ultimate and unconditional and free of the demands of the one God.

The unity of God is also, in fact, the ground of any morality at all. If reality is not ultimately rooted in one single source, maintained in harmony by one undivided power, and given its meaning by one coherent horizon, then there is no authority that can claim unconditional allegiance. In a polytheistic view of the world there can be loyalty to a particular power and there can be law sanctioned by a particular society and structure, but these can never be unconditional either in their guarantee of protection or in their claims on the individual's obedience. They are always relative to the power structure and to an individual's position within it. Only in a monotheistic view of the world (that is, one which acknowledges one God alone) can there be unconditional claims that go beyond the external force of sanctions to the internal force of conscience, and that is where morality is founded. It is the unconditional claim of God's rule and kingship as creator, provider and source of all meaning and purpose that constitutes an absolute exigence arising within the innermost freedom of the human person and summoning forth the authentic realization of that innermost freedom. Freedom is more than random selection. Freedom is purposeful, moving toward the attainment of an adequate and fulfilling goal. That is why freedom is created by the very exigence (that is, by the demands, laws) of the one God in relation to whom all things make sense and find their fulfillment.

The unity of God has yet another aspect of practical importance. Only if the world and all that exists is the creation of one God to whom all things relate back and by whose power and wisdom all is sustained can one expect to find an ultimate and overarching harmony in the disparate forces of the world of nature and human affairs. Only on this condition can one expect to find a "covenant" in creation that expresses the fidelity of God in the drawing of all things to fulfillment in his purpose. Only on this condition can one expect to find a faithful correspondence between human observation, reason, knowledge and wisdom on the one hand and the wisdom and law by which the natural universe is patterned on the other. In other words, it is really only within a faith in one God, omnipotent and omniprovident, that human science can be founded with confidence that it leads to truth and is reliable. Only in the context of such faith in one God can one assume that truth is one, and therefore that there really is such a thing as truth.

A final practical consequence of faith in the one God is the inseparability of love of God from love of neighbor and the universality of the claims of love of neighbor which never offer grounds for the exclusion of anyone. In a polytheistic view of the world loyalty may be to one group and responsibility for the welfare of that group only. Persons of another class, race, culture or national grouping may be excluded from concern and care if attitudes, values and behavior are determined by a reciprocal relationship with a tribal or partisan deity in a polytheistic world. But in a monotheistic world, all are the creatures of the one Creator who made them interdependent in pursuit of his unified purpose in his creation. Their very interdependence is his creation and his will. There can be no positive response to God the Creator which does not accept this interdependence and the responsibility for all others which it implies. There can be no real freedom except the joint freedom of a non-exclusive community of human persons.

Such is the God of Israel whom Jesus called his Father. Israel pictured this God as fighting his people's battles, being angered and sad and disappointed over his people's infidelities, having arguments with Satan the tempter or holding consultations with the court of heaven. At the same time the Hebrew Bible, most particularly in the psalms, expresses the transcendent holiness of God whom no one has ever counseled, who is beholden to none nor in need of anything human beings can offer, the wisdom of whose provident plans is beyond scrutiny. This God is spoken of as Father but described often enough in mothering terms. Rabbinic literature describes him not only as the lawgiver but as one who delightedly studies the law. Moreover, Hebrew thought is not content with the picture of solitary eminence and splendor evoked by the insistence on the unity of God, but personifies the Torah or law, as well as the Wisdom of God and sometimes the Spirit or breath of God. These personifications allow for divine conversations and divine relationships in the stories told by the rabbis of the Talmud (the ancient compilation of the commentary on the law, known simply as the Teaching).

The Christian experience of God begins with the prayer of Jesus into which he drew his followers of all generations in time. In that prayer the followers of Jesus certainly find the majesty and power, the holiness and unplumbed depths of silence of the transcendent God who is before all things and beyond all things and inscrutable. But much more prominently in that prayer the followers of Jesus experience the immanence of God in the tender and comfortable intimacy of Jesus with the Father. It is in that familial style that Christians find the divine conversations and the divine relationships that break into the picture of solitary eminence and splendor. Jesus is not simply an onlooker or one who listens in to the divine conversations. He is within the conversation. In his person he is the Wisdom of God "playing in the world" and speaking the human reality of the world to the transcendence of God as well as giving utterance to the silent, transcendent God in a concrete presence in the world. Jesus is in his person the law that proceeds from the Father as lawgiver but which the Father himself delightedly studies. Christians therefore see the relationship between Jesus and the Father not only as something that has occurred within the contingencies of history, but as the historical expression of the reality that is the very being of God. In the relationship between Jesus and the Father time and contingency sink away. What Jesus is and expresses in the particular historical situation in his human life is one with the timeless and pre-existent reality of the Word or self-utterance of God's unbegotten being—that eternal, pre-existent reality of the Word that is already expressed in creation itself with its harmony and its imaging of God.

The Christian experience of God, then, begins with the prayer of Jesus into which he draws them so that they may share his Spirit which becomes their Spirit and their life—his own Spirit, the Holy Spirit which is the very breath of God that hovered over the chaos of uncreation and came especially to quicken the human person in the creation and came again and again to arouse the prophetic voice, the healing hand, the saving deed. As his followers observe Jesus in conversation with the Father, that Spirit is at the same time the bond between the two and a third in the conversation. The Spirit is to continue the conversation and carry it further into the world, transforming creation, when Jesus has returned to the Father. This Spirit breathes the transcendent being and life of God into creation. It *is* the very breathing and life of God. But it is also another partner in the divine conversation in which the embodied life of God in creation reaches back to the transcendence of God in a sigh of love and longing that constitutes unity in plurality. Christians know this from their experience because this Spirit breathes in them as their own life but as something deeper than their own life that brings them to quickening at a new level of intensity of being beyond themselves. Christians know this and know that they stand in the presence of mystery, in the presence of the mystery of God. They know also that the Spirit of God that dwells in them and gives new life to the community that is now the body of Jesus in the world is one with that life and love which are in the timeless inner reality of God himself.

Gradually Christians came to include the Spirit in their prayers in such a way that the binitarian forms which linked Jesus to the Father in Christian worship gave way more and more to trinitarian forms in speaking of God, naming Father, Son and Holy Spirit. Certainly in their worship Christians did not intend to abandon faith in the one God of Israel. Equally obviously they wanted to express in its fullness their experience of God in the Christian community and the trinitarian form that that experience of God had in fact taken. The expressions of a trinitarian perception of God in worship preceded dogmatic formulations and have their own validity independently of the later dogmatic formulations. Yet, as in so many matters, the Church was simply not allowed (by historical circumstances and the questions arising from them) to leave its teachings in the suggestive poetic language of prayer in which it was best expressed. Interpretations came up which had to be repudiated. There were explanations offered which were frankly tritheistic (simply opted for three gods); there were also explanations which tended to lose the distinction between Jesus and the Father, and there were others which made of the Son an intermediate being neither divine nor human. Such attempts to rationalize the Christian vision forced theologians, bishops and councils to attempt an explanation which could become official and which would preserve the mystery intact in a formula that would incorporate the paradoxical elements and not try to resolve them.

The trinitarian doctrine of Christians might have been expressed in a number of ways. The language that found favor was that which had been used in Christology, that is, in the attempts to formulate who Christians understood Jesus to be. This was the language of three "persons" and one "substance" or "nature." This language dates at least from the fourth century and had become general and official by the sixth. Until our own times it was questioned very little after that early formulation. Certainly the Church Fathers who bequeathed this to us intended to convey the idea of relationship in the oneness of God such that relationships of human persons to God and human persons among themselves were to be seen as a reflection or mirroring of the love of God. Equally certainly, the Church Fathers did not intend "person" in the modern sense taken literally. That would simply mean three gods. There are aspects of human person-hood that are relevant and intended in this use of the word, and other aspects that are not. In any case, the word "person" is an abstraction drawn from the human individuals we know. To apply the term to God is necessarily analogy. It is an important analogy, because we in our human experience and language have only two categories, personal and impersonal (which means less than personal). Of these two, God is certainly more appropriately represented by personal analogies. Yet modern authors have suggested that some term suggesting "beyond personality" would be even more appropriate.

If the term "person" applied to God is necessarily analogous, this is even more true of the expression "three persons." What is involved in the end is the irreducible mystery, the insoluble paradox. For this we have another quite official formulation which is possibly much less likely to mislead contemporary readers and listeners. The Athanasian Creed, which does not seem to stem from Athanasius despite its commonly used name but which probably dates from the fifth or sixth century, offers this other formula: "We worship one God in Trinity and Trinity in unity." Although this Creed goes on to offer the explanation in terms of persons and substance, it is not really necessary and not really possible to put precise and unequivocal content into the terms "Trinity" and "unity." Any content that can be given them remains in the realm of analogy.

Yet the mystery of the Triune God is at the heart of Christian faith, for Christians believe that God is revealed to them in their historical experience. If God is not really what this revelation shows God to be, then the Christian revelation does not carry its believers any farther than each person's own imagination and projection. The whole Christian faith depends on the truthfulness and trustworthiness of Jesus and his apostolic witnesses, not only when they testify to their own experiences but also when they testify to the God who is revealed to them and through them to the world.

Thus the Christian faith begins and ends in God. It begins with the self-revelation of God and it ends with the reality of the God who is revealed, while the manner and process of the revelation takes in the whole sweep of human history and the whole range of human experience, gathered up in Jesus Christ and brought back into focus so that "God may be all in all."

Related Material

Besides the official Church teachings which may be found in The Teaching of the Catholic Church *by J. Neuner and H. Roos (Alba House), some other contemporary writings may be helpful in understanding the Christian doctrine of God. The historical development is sketched briefly by John H. Wright in the section on* God *of* An American Catholic Catechism *(Seabury). The problems in the understanding of the doctrine are explained through the study of modern authors by Charles Bent,* Interpreting the Doctrine of God *(Paulist Press). A particularly helpful reflection on the traditional formulations is offered in Part I of the* Introduction to Christianity *by Josef Ratzinger (Herder/Seabury).*

Index